The Cato Institute

The Cato Institute is named for the libertarian pamphlets, *Cato's Letters,* which were inspired by the Roman Stoic, Cato the Younger. Written by John Trenchard and Thomas Gordon, *Cato's Letters* were widely read in the American colonies in the early eighteenth century and played a major role in laying the philosophical foundation for the revolution that followed.

The erosion of civil and economic liberties in the modern world has occurred in concert with a widening array of social problems. These disturbing developments have resulted from a major failure to examine social problems in terms of the fundamental principles of human dignity, economic welfare, and justice.

The Cato Institute aims to broaden public policy debate by sponsoring programs designed to assist both the scholar and the concerned layperson in analyzing questions of political economy.

The programs of the Cato Institute include the sponsorship and publication of basic research in social philosophy and public policy; publication of major journals on the scholarship of liberty and commentary on political affairs; production of debate forums for radio; and organization of an extensive program of symposia, seminars, and conferences.

CATO INSTITUTE
1700 Montgomery Street
San Francisco, California 94111

The Fallacy of the Mixed Economy

The Fallacy of the Mixed Economy

An "Austrian" Critique of Conventional Economics and Government Policy

Stephen C. Littlechild

With a Foreword by Richard E. Wagner

CATO PAPER No. 2

INSTITUTE
San Francisco, California

Publisher's Note: This *Cato Paper* was originally published in June 1978 by The Institute of Economic Affairs, London, as Hobart Paper No. 80. The present edition has been revised for the American reader.

Printed in the United States of America.

CATO INSTITUTE
1700 Montgomery Street
San Francisco, California 94111

CONTENTS

ACKNOWLEDGMENTS

I should like to express my indebtedness to the following, without whom this *Paper* could never have been written: the editor of the London *City Press*, whose pages alone in 1961 carried the banner of Mises and Hayek; Professor Jack Wiseman, who convinced me that cost is subjective; Professors Israel Kirzner and Ludwig Lachmann, who patiently answered my questions on Austrian economics; the Earhart Foundation, which supported my visit to New York University to write a first draft of this discussion; Professor Terence Hutchison, Sudha Shenoy, and Glyn Picton who, in addition to Professors Kirzner and Wiseman, contributed helpful written comments on the final draft (almost all of which have been incorporated, but responsibility for any remaining errors and omissions unfortunately rests with me); Arthur Seldon, who provided patient editorial guidance; Kathy Major, who cheerfully typed so beautifully what must have seemed an endless series of drafts; and my wife, Kate, who throughout had to bear the consequences, if not the costs, of my writing this *Paper*.

April 1978   S.C.L.

FOREWORD

Stephen C. Littlechild's *The Fallacy of the Mixed Economy* sets forth the central principles of Austrian economics and examines the implications of these principles for government policy toward business. Littlechild lists four differentiae of Austrian economics: subjectivism, methodological individualism, the attachment of particular importance to the passage of time, and a recognition that social institutions that serve the common welfare are more often the unintended product of human action than the intended product of legislation.

While Littlechild distinguishes Austrian economics by these four differentiae, there are a striking number of economists, past and present, whose central understanding of economics is largely congruent with these differentiae, but who do not appear on the lists of economists to whom the adjective "Austrian" is applied. Among past economists, such names as Frank Knight, Frank A. Fetter, Herbert J. Davenport, Knut Wicksell, and Philip Wicksteed, along with Oskar Morgenstern and Joseph Schumpeter, are but a fraction of those who come to mind. I would wager that the number of economists who would affirm the essential validity of Littlechild's four differentiae is considerably larger than the number who would consciously classify themselves as "Austrian" economists. The acceptance of these differentiae as a point of departure for economic analysis is far more important than the adoption of an identifying adjective. Nonetheless, for linguistic ease, I shall refer to Austrian economics and neoclassical economics to signify respectively an acceptance and a rejection of Littlechild's four differentiae.

Austrian economics is perhaps most noted for, and rejected because of, its opposition to the positivistic testing of economic theory. Being realists rather than nominalists, Austrian economists strive to articulate universally valid principles and to deduce the implications of those principles. As Littlechild notes, the law of demand is such a principle. It cannot be tested because any failure of it to hold can be attributed to changes in other relevant factors. For instance, income may rise at the same time the price rises. Alternatively, the buyer may have broken a leg and may find it easier to pay a higher price to have milk delivered than to continue to travel to a store to buy it more cheaply.

Economic theory is a system of logic, not a set of propositions to be tested. Nonetheless, Austrian economics offers substantial scope for empirical-historical research, although its focus is different from that of neoclassical economics. For instance, monetary changes will have important economic consequences. A theory of these consequences can be developed from Austrian theory. A judgment about applicability of this theory, however, must be based on empirical-historical research. Austrian economics, therefore, does not deny the value of empirical research, for such research is vital to a concrete understanding of our present age, or of any other age.

Government policy toward industry is dominated by the idea of the mixed economy. The market economy is seen as inherently defective because it does not correspond to some textbook notion of perfect competition, and the task of government is seen as one of intervention to correct these defects. The idea of the mixed economy is illustrated in a variety of classroom exercises employing standard neoclassical comparative statics. For instance, a competitve industry in equilibrium can be compared with a monopolist, and the welfare loss resulting from the monopoly can be shaded with colored chalk. In this familiar exercise there is no problem of knowledge of such things as consumer demands and techniques of production because the professor presumes possession of the knowledge in the very construction of the problem. Neither is there any question of the introduction of new products or techniques of production because the method of comparative statics prevents such actions. Nor is there any question of incentive, for, in addition to their omniscience, professors are always benevolent; merely to show the amount of welfare loss is sufficient to elicit the appropriate policy response. But most especially, no consideration is given to the means by which an economy can calculate moves from one state of equilibrium to another; nor, more important still, is consideration given to the way in which actual economic shifts occur in a world where such equilibrium states do not and cannot exist.

But where does the knowledge necessary to improve the situation come from? The Austrian emphasis on the market process as a means of producing knowledge shows the danger of misapplying the neoclassical framework. The knowledge that economists take for granted in their classroom teaching is itself produced within the market process and is unobtainable outside that process—as the debate on collectivist planning a half-century ago revealed. Moreover, what is the incentive of the regulator in the mixed economy? The professor has an incentive to avoid the embarrassment of being caught by his students in an error of logic. But the classroom-type "knowledge" is not available in reality, so such a form of incentive cannot operate. Indeed, as an increasing volume of modern research is showing, political success can be enhanced by actions that actually diminish economic prosperity. Professor Littlechild explains quite nicely how Austrian economics avoids the fallacy of the mixed economy.

While Littlechild's monograph was originally written for a British audience, there is much of value for American readers, for many American applications could easily be developed. Antitrust policy, with the renewed attack upon business by the Federal Trade Commission and the Department of Justice, is understood quite differently in light of the Austrian insights. This attack, rationalized by the neoclassical approach to the theory of perfect competition, is found in such proposals as that to ban all mergers involving sales or assets exceeding $2 billion, unless the merger can be proved both to have no anticompetitive effects and to produce tangible economic benefits. It is also found in the attack on dominant firms, as well as in the development of the idea of shared monopoly.

Patent policy, the idea of monopolistic competition, unionism, government enterprise, and public regulation are other instances where the Austrian perspective yields uniquely valuable insights. The Department of Energy, for instance, is still with us, as is our energy problem. We can feel assured that the problem will remain so long as the department remains; the direction of causation, however, is the reverse of what official Washington would have us believe. The reader of Littlechild's volume will be able to understand the truly fraudulent nature of the purported energy crisis. Professor Littlechild has done a remarkable job, in a volume of this brevity, both of making a contribution to specific issues of public policy and of indicating some desirable redirection of the research agenda of economics.

February 1979

Richard E. Wagner
Blacksburg, Virginia

Introduction

This discussion attempts to answer two questions: What is "Austrian economics"? What does Austrian economics have to say about government policy on industry today?

The Austrian tradition provides an approach to economic theory quite distinct from that of what might be called the "neo-classical mainstream," i.e., economics as it has developed since 1870 at the hands of such leading European figures as Jevons and Walras, Marshall and Pigou, and more recently American economists like Professors Paul Samuelson and Kenneth Arrow. It is this approach which is embodied in almost all introductory and intermediate textbooks, not least in Samuelson's *Economics*, and which constitutes common ground to a wide section of the economics profession. It is, however, an approach that is proving increasingly embarrassing, mainly because it is unable to analyze many phenomena in the real world that are associated with incomplete knowledge and uncertainty.

Almost all the advice that governments have received from economists during the past half-century has naturally come from this neoclassical "mainstream." Policy recommendations have differed, but the general consensus seems to have been that countries like the United States and Britain need a "mixed" economy of government and private activity in the market. There has been considerable experimenting in the "mix" of the mixture, but the government component has risen more or less steadily. In Britain, for example, according to provisional findings by government statisticians, the "public" sector's share of national wealth (i.e., that controlled *directly* by government) appears to have roughly trebled in the decade to 1975, from some 8 percent in 1966 to an estimated 26 percent in 1975.[1] In addition, almost all the activities of the private sector are subject to government regulation, influence, or scrutiny.

Economic theory cannot prescribe what government policy

[1] *Times* (London), 8 February 1978.

ought to be. It can only hope to ascertain what kinds of means *are or are not* suitable for attaining chosen ends. Since Austrian economic theory is so distinct from "mainstream" theory, we shall not be surprised to find that the implications for policy are quite different. It becomes apparent that, when imperfections of knowledge are taken into account, many institutions of the mixed economy, some novel and some familiar, are by no means well suited to the purposes that most economists, politicians, and laymen still fondly imagine them to be.

A Brief Summary

Neoclassical "mainstream" economics tends to see the economic problem facing society as one of efficiently allocating resources in the light of preferences, techniques, and resource availabilities, knowledge of which is supposed somehow to be "given." Austrian economics, by contrast, sees the problem as including the *discovery* of those preferences, techniques, and resource availabilities. Neoclassical economics finds it appropriate to view the economy as if it were in or near a *state* of equilibrium. Austrian economics sees the economy as involved in a continual *process* of discovery, coordination, and change.

These contrasting viewpoints lead to different interpretations of the role of government. Neoclassical "welfare" economists (i.e., those concerned with devising policies to optimize the use of resources) ask whether the market provides the right incentives to allocate resources efficiently. Where it does not—where they therefore say there is "market failure"—they see the case for government either to correct the incentives of the market or to replace the market entirely. Austrian economists, on the other hand, ask whether the market provides the right incentives to discover where there is scope for increased coordination leading to *improvements* in the allocation of resources. They are aware that the market frequently, indeed *always*, makes mistakes, but on the whole they conclude that the government cannot hope to acquire sufficient information to do a better job. They therefore ask what kind of government policies provide the most encouragement for the co-ordinating process of the market.

In concrete terms, neoclassical welfare economists have seen a requirement for antitrust legislation (and numerous bureaus, commissions, and agencies to implement such legislation), cost-benefit analyses, nationalized industries, and government economic planning as devices to correct "market failure" and improve resource allocation. Austrian economists have generally seen these institutions as more likely to *impede* the process of coordination. They have emphasized instead the importance of freedom of entry and the development of private property rights as means to encourage the smooth functioning of markets and the competitive process, and thereby to protect the public from exploitation and inefficiency, not only from monopoly but also from unnecessary government.

A Comparison of Textbooks

It may be helpful briefly to compare "neoclassical mainstream" and "Austrian" textbooks. A typical neoclassical textbook[2] emphasizes two central concepts: *maximization* of the utility of individuals or the profits of firms, and *equilibrium* between individuals and firms in markets and the economy as a whole. The analysis is conducted almost entirely on the assumption of perfect knowledge.

Austrian textbooks reject this latter assumption.[3] It follows that the concepts of maximization and equilibrium must be supplemented by the concept of individual *alertness to new knowledge* leading to adjustment processes in the market. From this new point of view, familiar notions such as "perfect" and "imperfect" competition no longer appear very helpful. It might be argued, therefore, that Austrian economics provides a *generalization* and *redirection of neoclassical thought*, rather than a "root and branch" replacement for it.

[2] For example, C. E. Ferguson and J. P. Gould, *Microeconomic Theory,* 4th ed. (Homewood, Ill.: Irwin, 1975), which is described by the authors as "a textbook on neoclassical price theory."
[3] M. N. Rothbard, *Man, Economy, and State: A Treatise on Economic Principles* (New York: Van Nostrand, 1962); I. M. Kirzner, *Market Theory and the Price System* (Princeton: Van Nostrand, 1963).

3

I. Who Are the Austrians?

The Growing Awareness

In 1974, Professor Friedrich Hayek was (jointly) awarded the Nobel Prize in Economics.[4] Hayek is nowadays accepted as the leader of the so-called Austrian School of Economics. Over the last three years there has been an increasing number of references, in the press and the economics literature, to this school of thought. *Business Week*, for example, has run two feature articles on the implications of Austrian ideas for macroeconomic policy. There have been several sessions on leading Austrians at professional economics meetings in the United States and, more recently, in Britain. A series of introductory weekend seminars in London and major American cities has attracted more than a thousand participants. Exponents of the Austrian approach have themselves been on lecture tours to many universities, and a series of reprints and original papers in Austrian economics is now under way, sponsored by the Cato Institute and the Institute for Humane Studies.

The economist in his thirties or forties now in industry, in civil service, or indeed in academia itself, must find all this puzzling. Austrian economics did not form part of his university courses, even as a postgraduate student—unless he was at the London School of Economics, where Hayek taught from 1931 to 1950. From his browsing in the literature he may associate with the Austrian School the work of Menger on marginal utility or Böhm-Bawerk on capital and interest, or Schumpeter on the "perennial gale of creative destruction" in the modern economy. But surely, he may feel, all these ideas have already been incorporated into

[4]Hayek's Nobel Memorial Lecture, entitled "The Pretense of Knowledge," was included with other essays in *Unemployment and Monetary Policy: Government as Generator of the "Business Cycle,"* Cato Paper no. 3 (San Francisco: Cato Institute, 1979).

5

"mainstream" theory?

To a large extent these ideas have indeed been accepted, but they by no means exhaust the Austrian tradition, nor indeed are they fully representative of it. Marginal utility played only one part in Menger's scheme of things, and the notion of marginal equalities was by no means as central as in later mathematical writers. We also now know that Menger considered Böhm-Bawerk's theory of capital and interest "one of the greatest errors ever committed."[5] As for Schumpeter, although an Austrian by origin, he espoused too many Walrasian beliefs[6] that were anathema to subsequent Austrians such as Mises to be accepted uncritically as one of the school.

What, then, *is* Austrian economics? What are its consequences for our understanding of the economy and for economic policy? Who are the Austrians anyway? The rest of this chapter will establish who the Austrians are. Chapter 2 gives a general outline of the Austrian position, and Chapter 3 a more detailed exposition of the Austrian theory of competition and the market process. The remaining chapters apply these Austrian insights to a broad range of topics where the question at issue is the appropriate role of government in industry.

To deal with all aspects of Austrian economics would require a very large book—or several books. Other studies deal with aspects of Austrian thought which by and large have been accepted into "mainstream" theory (the contribution of Austrian economics or economists to the history of economic thought) and with Austrian thinking on capital theory, money, credit, the trade cycle, unemployment, etc.[7] Austrian contributions here have been quite distinctive. On the economics of capital, for example, it has been

---

[5] J. A. Schumpeter, *History of Economic Analysis* (New York: Oxford University Press, 1954), p. 847, n. 8.

[6] For example, general equilibrium and mathematical economics.

[7] *See,* for example, L. M. Lachmann, *Macroeconomic Thinking and the Market Economy* (Menlo Park, Calif.: Institute for Humane Studies, 1978), and the following studies by F. A. Hayek: *A Tiger by the Tail: The Keynesian Legacy of Inflation,* Cato Paper no. 7 (San Francisco: Cato Institute, 1979); *Unemployment and Monetary Policy; Choice in Currency: A Way to Stop Inflation,* Institute of Economic Affairs Occasional Paper no. 48 (London, 1976); *Denationalisation of Money,* Institute of Economic Affairs Hobart Paper no. 70 (London, 1976).

argued that it is impossible to measure the size of the capital stock and, on the economics of money, that the *mode* by which money is injected into the economy, and not merely the total *quantity* of money, has a crucial effect on prices and production. Certainly, the three-pronged debate between Friedman, Hayek, and the neo-Keynesians on macroeconomic policy is still in full swing,[8] as illustrated in Hayek's recent and perhaps most radical work, *The Denationalization of Money*.

The Origin of the Austrian School

The "Austrian School of Economics" may be said to date from the publication in 1871 of Carl Menger's *Principles of Economics (Grundsätze der Volkswirtschaftslehre)*. It was not immediately acclaimed. "Until the end of the Seventies," remarked Mises, "there was no 'Austrian School.' There was only Carl Menger."[9] Subsequently, Menger (1840-1921) attracted a small but devoted band of disciples, notably Wieser (1851-1926) and Böhm-Bawerk (1851-1914), to expound and extend his thinking.

Menger's second book, *Investigations into the Method of Sociology and Political Economy,* appeared in 1883. It was intended as a defense of economics as a theoretical discipline, and represented a full scale attack on the aims and methods of historical economics as they had been developing in Germany. Gustav Schmoller, the leading member of the German historical school, reacted with a rather contemptuous review. The various publications engendered over the next two decades by this controversy are known as the *methodenstreit* or "clash over methods." It was during this clash that the term "Austrian School" was first used, in a derogatory sense, by members of the German historical school to refer to Menger and his disciples.

The Austrian School generated a rich crop of students, the best

---

[8] *See,* for example, Hayek, *Unemployment and Monetary Policy* and *Choice in Currency. See also* M. Friedman, *Unemployment versus Inflation?,* Institute of Economic Affairs Occasional Paper no. 44 (London, 1975) and *Inflation and Unemployment: The New Dimension of Politics,* Institute of Economic Affairs Occasional Paper no. 51 (London, 1977).

[9] L. von Mises, *The Historical Setting of the Austrian School of Economics* (New Rochelle, N.Y.: Arlington House, 1969), p. 10.

known of the second generation being Ludwig von Mises (1881-1973) and Joseph Schumpeter (1883-1950). The third generation, born around the turn of this century and taught by Mises, includes Haberler (b. 1901), Hayek (b. 1899), Machlup (b. 1902), Morgenstern (1902-1977), and Rosenstein-Rodan (b. 1902). All these economists eventually emigrated to the United States, and in one sense the Austrian School thereby came to an end.

It may be argued that the school had ended long before. By the turn of the century, the *methodenstreit* had petered out for lack of substantial disagreement, and Mises was later able to write:

> After some years all the essential ideas of the Austrian School were by and large accepted as an integral part of economic theory. About the time of Menger's demise (1921), one no longer distinguished between an Austrian School and other economics. The appellation "Austrian School" became the name given to an important chapter of the history of economic thought; it was no longer the name of a specific sect with doctrines different from those held by other economists.[10]

The Continuation of the Austrian School

How, then, did the concept of an Austrian School survive? Mises gave as the one exception to his generalization his own work on the course and causes of the trade cycle. In retrospect, we can see that subsequent "mainstream" economic theory developed along lines which differed in several crucial respects from those envisaged by Menger. Consequently, "mainstream" economics failed to incorporate the bulk of the ideas of Mises and Hayek, who of all the Austrians worked most closely in the tradition of Menger.

It is possible, then, to speak of a distinct Austrian tradition even after 1920 in the sense of the ideas and methods initially proposed by Carl Menger and developed by Mises and Hayek. Several economists, regardless of their place of birth or education, have consciously worked in this tradition. It is in this sense that Ludwig Lachmann, a Berliner who studied under Hayek at the London School of Economics in the 1930s, and Israel Kirzner and Murray Rothbard, who both attended Mises's seminar in New York in the 1950s and 1960s, are now considered

[10]Ibid., p. 41.

current members of the historically recognized Austrian School.

The last few years have seen a resurgence of interest in the Austrian approach. Younger scholars teaching in universities throughout the United States include Walter Block, Roger W. Garrison, Walter E. Grinder, Gerald P. O'Driscoll, Jr., Mario J. Rizzo, and a further half-dozen graduate students at New York University. Indeed, New York is effectively the headquarters of the Austrian School today! It should be mentioned, however, that the Carl Menger Society in London runs a regular seminar program on Austrian ideas; that Erich Streissler, the current holder of Menger's chair in Vienna, appears to have sympathy with the traditional Austrian approach; and that there is emerging interest in Australia, encouraged by Sudha Shenoy, a British "Austrian" of Indian origin.

Related Writers

Our account would not be complete without some reference to other writers who have been particularly influenced, directly or indirectly, by the ideas of the Austrian School. Early followers included Smart and Wicksteed in Britain, Irving Fisher and Frank Fetter in the United States, Cossa and Pantaleoni in Italy, and Wicksell in Sweden.[11] Later, Lord Robbins, Sir John Hicks, and others at the London School of Economics were influential in spreading Austrian ideas within Britain.[12]

Professor G. L. S. Shackle was a student of Hayek's at the London School of Economics, and it has been remarked that to a striking extent Mises and Shackle share a common outlook on the foundations of economics.[13] Professor Brian Loasby (Stirling

[11] I am indebted to Fritz Machlup for these suggestions.

[12] L. C. Robbins, *An Essay on the Nature and Significance of Economic Science* (London: Macmillan, 1971), especially pp. 106-8; J. R. Hicks, *Capital and Time: A Neo-Austrian Theory* (Oxford: Clarendon Press, 1973). It may be noted, however, that Kirzner has taken issue with Robbins's emphasis on "economizing" to the exclusion of "alertness" (below, p. 22) and that even Hicks's "neo-Austrian" approach is associated rather narrowly with the Böhm-Bawerkian theory of capital.

[13] L. M. Lachmann, "From Mises to Shackle: An Essay," *Journal of Economic Literature,* March 1976, pp. 54-62. An example of Shackle's work is *Epistemics and Economics* (Cambridge: At the University Press, 1972).

University) and Dr. Alan Coddington (Queen Mary College, London) have in their turn been influenced by Shackle.[14] G. F. Thirlby (London School of Economics, retired) and Professor Jack Wiseman (London School of Economics, now at York) reflect a distinctive London School of Economics tradition which can ultimately be traced via Robbins and Hayek to Mises and the earlier Austrians.[15] G. B. Richardson, a student of Hicks at Oxford in the 1940s, has also acknowledged the important influence of Hayek's writings.[16] Nevertheless, these British writers have not worked consciously in the Austrian tradition, and in some respects they have gone further than the Austrians in emphasizing the unpredictability of economic events and the limited role of general equilibrium.

Since Hayek taught for nearly two decades at the University of Chicago, albeit not in the economics department, one would expect to find there traces of his influence. Members of the so-called Chicago School generally share a somewhat similar philosophic outlook but differ sharply from the Austrians on methodology. I shall argue later, nevertheless, that the work of Professors Armen Alchian and Harold Demsetz, both formerly of Chicago but now at the University of California at Los Angeles (UCLA), in many respects runs parallel to that of the Austrians. So too, in a different way, does that of the "Virginia School" writers on public choice, notably Professors J. M. Buchanan and Gordon Tullock, both of whom also studied at Chicago.[17]

---

[14]B. J. Loasby, *Choice, Complexity and Ignorance* (Cambridge: At the University Press, 1976); Alan Coddington, "The Rationale of General Equilibrium Theories," *Economic Inquiry,* December 1975, pp. 539-58.

[15]See J. M. Buchanan, *Cost and Choice* (Chicago: Markham, 1969), and J. M. Buchanan and G. F. Thirlby, *London School of Economics Essays on Cost* (London: Weidenfeld & Nicolson, 1973). *See also* J. Wiseman, "Costs and Decisions" (Paper delivered to the Association of University Teachers of Economics at the University of York, March 1978).

[16]G. B. Richardson, *Information and Investment* (London: Oxford University Press, 1960).

[17]A. A. Alchian and W. R. Allen, *University Economics,* 3rd ed. (London: Prentice Hall, 1974); H. Demsetz, "Information and Efficiency: Another Viewpoint," *Journal of Law and Economics,* April 1969, pp. 1-22; J. M. Buchanan and G. Tullock, *The Calculus of Consent* (Ann Arbor: University of Michigan Press, 1962) and several other works.

II. Austrian Ideas

The Views of Carl Menger

Menger is probably best known as one of the coinitiators (with Jevons and Walras) of the "marginal" or "subjective" revolution of the 1870s. This revolution, as Lachmann has remarked, amounted to a recognition that "value is not a property inherent in goods, but constitutes a relationship between an appraising mind and the object appraised.[18] Hence, there arose the need systematically to introduce *subjective* utility into economics. Some would argue that, for Menger, subjectivism meant essentially that different men have different tastes; recent work by Kirzner and others has emphasized the degree to which Menger's work contained at least the seeds of recognition of the role of knowledge and expectations.

Menger also emphasized what he called the "atomistic" method. The nation as a whole is not equivalent to *one* large decision-maker, but is rather composed of a complex *collection* of individual decision-makers.

> Whoever wants to understand theoretically the phenomena of a national economy . . . must for this reason attempt to go back to their *true* elements, *to the individual economies in the nation* [i.e., to the individual decision-makers], and to investigate the laws by which the former are built up from the latter.[19]

The classical economists, Menger felt, had failed to do this.

---

[18] L. M. Lachmann, "Methodological Individualism and the Market Economy," in *Roads to Freedom: Essays in Honour of Friedrich A. Von Hayek,* ed. Erich Streissler (London: Routledge and Kegan Paul, 1969), p. 95.

[19] C. Menger, *Problems of Economics and Sociology* [1883] (Urbana: University of Illinois Press, 1960), p. 93.

To explain some of these phenomena was for Menger one of the major tasks of economics.

> Language, religion, law, even the state itself, and, to mention a few economic and social phenomena, the phenomena of markets, of competition, of money, and numerous other social structures are already met within epochs of history *where we cannot properly speak of a purposeful activity of the community*, as such, directed at establishing them.
>
> We are confronted here with the appearance of social institutions which to a high degree serve the welfare of society. Indeed, they are not infrequently of vital significance for the latter and yet are *not the result of communal activity*. It is here that we meet a noteworthy, perhaps the most noteworthy, problem of the social sciences: How can it be that institutions which serve the common welfare and are extremely significant for its development come into being *without a common will directed towards establishing them?*[20] (My italics.)

Menger used the term "organic" to refer to phenomena generated by such processes, as opposed to "pragmatic" phenomena which are the result of legislation or agreement to that conscious end. Here, too, he felt that the classical economists had failed to appreciate this distinction.

> What Adam Smith and even those of his followers who have most successfully developed political economy can actually be charged with is . . . their defective understanding of the *unintentionally created social institutions* and their significance for economy. It is the opinion appearing chiefly in their writings that the institutions of economy are always the *intended* product of the common will of society as such, results of expressed agreement of members of society or of positive legislation. . . . The result is that the broad realm of unintentionally created social structures remains closed to their theoretical comprehension.[21] (My italics.)

These three concepts emphasized by Menger—subjective utility, the atomistic method, and organic phenomena—form the basis for the distinctive Austrian tradition which continued after 1920.

---

[20] Ibid., p. 146.
[21] Ibid., p. 172.

Developments of Later Generations

Modern Austrian economics is sometimes described as "thorough-going subjectivism." In Hayek's opinion, "It is probably no exaggeration to say that every important advance in economic theory during the last hundred years was a further step in the consistent application of subjectivism."[22] This was a development, he suggested, which had most consistently been carried out by Mises.

Neoclassical economics embodies individual tastes described in the form of charts called "indifference curves" but, for the most part, has not gone further in characterizing personalities. In Pareto's words: "The individual can disappear, providing he leaves us this photograph of his tastes."[23] If the purpose is to analyze the properties of general equilibrium in a state of perfect knowledge, this may suffice. But Austrian economics, in sharp contrast to neoclassical economics, has always attempted to explain behavior in a world characterized by lack or dispersion of knowledge. It has consequently been necessary to emphasize the importance of incorporating many other aspects of the individual personality, notably (a) *knowledge* about one's own tastes and the opportunities available; (b) *interpretations* of current events and the actions of others; (c) *expectations* about further events and behavior; and (d) *alertness* to new opportunities previously un-perceived.

What is important here, of course, is that people *differ* with respect to their knowledge, interpretations, expectations, and alertness. Subjectivism thus takes on a wider meaning than merely tastes, and Austrian economists have thereby been led to examine

> . . . the new problems which these developments [in subjectivism] make appear more and more central, such as the problem of the compatibility of intentions and expectations of different people, of the division of knowledge between them, and the process by which the relevant knowledge is acquired and expectations formed.[24]

[22] F. A. Hayek, *The Counter-Revolution of Science* (New York: Free Press, 1964), p. 31.

[23] V. Pareto, *Manual of Political Economy* [1906] (Fairfield, N.J.: Kelley, 1971), p. 120.

[24] Hayek, *Counter-Revolution of Science,* p. 33.

Methodological Individualism

Menger's "atomistic method" would nowadays be referred to as "methodological individualism." This is the consistent use of the intelligible conduct of individuals as building blocks from which to construct "models" of complex phenomena. It might be thought that "mainstream" economics, based as it is upon the decisions of individual producers and consumers, already fully embodies the principle of methodological individualism. It is not difficult to find important exceptions.

1. Despite much discussion of equilibrium prices, leading to a presumption that they occur, neoclassical economics does not explain *how*, in practice, they come about.

2. If the "firm" is not just a single entrepreneur but a collection of cooperating individuals, neoclassical economics does not explain how, or to what extent, the members of the firm, each with their own tasks and objectives, combine to design and carry out the firm's policy.

3. Economists often invoke a "social welfare function" which purports to embody the preferences of society, but welfare economics does not explain how the possibly conflicting beliefs and preferences of the individual members of society are aggregated to form this function.

4. Welfare economics tacitly assumes that a government policy, once decided upon, is correctly and efficiently carried out. It does not refer at all to the problems of designing a suitable organizational framework within which to coordinate and monitor the politicians and bureaucrats selected for the task.

In other words, "mainstream" economics has failed to relate the actions taken by these organizations to the preferences, knowledge, interpretations, expectations, and plans of their constituent members. The result has been that traditional theory has failed adequately to explain the behavior of such organizations. As we shall see, its "normative" prescriptions on what governments *should* do, especially concerning optimal policy for industry or government, have turned out to be naive or impracticable.

Unintended Consequences and the Passage of Time

It is a common view, which Mises shared, that the task of economics is to look beyond the immediate and obvious consequences of any action to the more distant and obscure consequences, which can only be appreciated by an understanding of economic theory. Hayek went further: He said the major task of economics (indeed, of the social sciences generally) is to explain "the unintended consequences of human action." Many social institutions, as Menger had realized, are "the results of human action but not of human design." This insight, as we shall see, has important implications for the appropriate role of government in society.

One further aspect of Austrian economics is especially important. Organic phenomena such as money and markets can be developed only by a process that takes place over time. The individuals who comprise an organization can form a common plan only by negotiations over time. Changes in knowledge and plans have significance only when earlier periods are compared with later ones. We thus see that an appreciation of the role of time—more precisely, the *passage* of time—is the fourth vital element of the Austrian approach, in addition to the concepts of subjectivism, methodological individualism, and organic phenomena.

It may be felt that the concept "Austrian" is still rather indistinct around the edges. This is no doubt true. It certainly cannot be claimed, for example, that Austrians alone saw the importance of introducing imperfect knowledge, expectations, learning, and time into economics. In the period up to 1929, F. H. Knight, J. M. Keynes, and the Scandinavian writers Wicksell, Myrdal, and Lindahl certainly emphasized one or more of these aspects.[25] In the last decade many eminent mathematical economists have attempted to develop theories of general equilibrium under uncertainty.[26] What can be claimed, perhaps, is that Austrian writers have pursued the implications of subjectivism

[25] *See* T. W. Hutchinson, *A Review of Economic Doctrines 1870-1929* (Oxford: Clarendon Press, 1953), especially chap. 20.

[26] *See* chap. 3 below, subsection entitled "Temporary Equilibrium Models."

with a significantly greater consciousness and consistency than other writers.

Austrian Methodology: Reservations about Empirical Testing

It is safe to say that no two Austrians have ever completely agreed on methodology, any more than have any two other economists. Nevertheless, there has been broad agreement on a general position, which Kirzner has summarized:

> Austrian economists are subjectivists; they emphasize the purposefulness of human action; they are unhappy with constructions that emphasize equilibrium to the exclusion of market processes; they are deeply suspicious of attempts to apply measurement procedures to economics; they are skeptical of empirical "proofs" of economic theorems and consequently have serious reservations about the validity and importance of a good deal of the empirical work being carried on in the economics profession today.[27]

This position is evidently quite different from that taken by "mainstream" economists. It is therefore necessary to provide a brief explanation.

It is nowadays widely held, and most emphatically taught at the University of Chicago, that economic laws and theories can be established only by adopting the methods of the natural sciences, such as physics. These proceed by inventing, testing, and revising hypotheses about the nature of, say, the atoms that are presumed to comprise familiar objects such as tables and chairs. Consequently, it is suggested, economists should make hypotheses about the ways in which "atoms" such as consumers, firms, governments, and economies make decisions, then test the predictions of these hypotheses against observed behavior. The adequacy of a theory should then be judged by how well it *predicts* behavior, rather than by how realistic its assumptions are. Indeed, it would be argued that the only test of realism *is* the test of pre-

---

[27] I. M. Kirzner, "On the Method of Austrian Economics," in *The Foundations of Modern Austrian Economics,* ed. E. G. Dolan (Kansas City: Sheed & Ward, 1976), p. 40.

diction. It is this behavioristic approach which has come to be known as "positive economics," and which is reflected in the title of one of the most respected introductory textbooks today.[28] The implication is that approaches to economics which do not follow this methodology are unscientific.

As the above quotation from Kirzner suggests, Austrians do not subscribe to this view. At least four reasons can be identified.

First, Austrians from Menger onwards (and indeed other economists such as Frank Knight) have always maintained that in observing the actions of other persons we are assisted by a capacity of *understanding* the meaning of such actions in a way in which we cannot understand physical events. Being human ourselves, we have insights into the behavior of other human beings which it is, in part, the task of the social sciences to explain.[29] We know, for example, that men are *purposeful* and that they are *alert to new possibilities* for increasing their satisfaction. They take *initiatives;* they do not merely *respond* passively to external stimuli in the way that biological organisms do. Thus, if we see a government pass a series of measures controlling prices and incomes, we may be led to correlate the actions taken with, say, the levels of inflation and unemployment precisely because of our suspicion that the government is actively trying to find a solution to what it perceives as a serious problem. The existence of such a sense of purpose we know, and do not need to *deduce* from observed behavior. Indeed, it might be argued that we *cannot* deduce it merely from observed behavior, and furthermore that any explanation or theory of observed behavior is ultimately unsatisfactory unless it is consistent with such knowledge.

The second Austrian reservation is based on the truth that it is difficult to make precise, testable predictions in situations where there is a large number of elements ("variables") about which it will never be possible to obtain the necessary full information.

---

[28] M. Friedman, *Essays in Positive Economics* (Chicago: University of Chicago Press, 1953), pp. 3-43. *See also* R. G. Lipsey, *An Introduction to Positive Economics* (London: Weidenfeld and Nicolson, 1963).

[29] Hayek, *Counter-Revolution of Science,* p. 25. Mises used the term *praxeology* to describe the sciences of human action, of which economics was the most developed.

This is, of course, the usual case in the social sciences. The economist will typically be able to predict only general *patterns* of behavior and not the behavior of each *individual* element. He can predict, for example, that a rise in price will lead to a fall in demand, but he cannot usually predict the exact extent of this change in demand, simply because he never has sufficient information about the preferences and opportunities of the individuals in question. He is limited, as Professor Hayek put it, to "prediction in principle" rather than "prediction in detail."[30] To insist that the only acceptable theories are those referring to measurable and testable magnitudes may cause the true theory to be disregarded and may lead to policies which make matters worse, as Hayek believes to be true of the present very serious problem of inflation and unemployment.[31]

Third, it is not even clear that economic theory *can* be empirically tested. Consider the "law of demand" just referred to, namely, that a rise in price will lead to a fall in demand. How is this law established? Many economists argue that we believe the law because it is continually being tested and has never been found false. If a rise in the price of, say, apples is occasionally followed by a *rise* in the demand for apples, they explain that consumers must have thought the higher-priced apples were of better quality, whereas the law applies only to apples perceived as identical. In this case, however, it seems that empirical testing established not the truth or falsity of the law of demand, *but whether the observer has correctly identified identical commodities.* How, then, is it ever possible to establish empirically the law of demand?

The fourth reservation about empirical work is based upon the Austrian insight that *there is an indeterminacy and unpredictability inherent in human preferences, human expectations, and human knowledge.* Shackle and Lachmann, in particular, have

---

[30]F. A. Hayek, *Studies in Philosophy, Politics and Economics* (Chicago: University of Chicago Press, 1967), pp. 22-42. Cf. Aristotle: "For it is the mark of an educated mind to expect that amount of exactness in each kind which the nature of the particular subject admits" (*Nicomachean Ethics* 1094b24).

[31]Hayek, "The Pretense of Knowledge," in *Unemployment and Monetary Policy,* part 2.

stressed the spontaneity and creativity of the act of choice. If this is true, one cannot hope to find *permanent* empirical regularities in economics which may be safely extrapolated beyond the existing data at hand to yield scientific theorems of universal validity. "Elasticities" of demand (the degree to which demand changes in response to changes in price) and substitution will remain constant only until such time as people discover new tastes or opportunities. There can be no unchanging "parameters" in the social sciences of the kind existing in the natural sciences.[32]

For these four reasons, Austrians argue that the nature of the social sciences is fundamentally different from that of the natural sciences. Economics as a social science requires a different methodology from physics. This is not at all "unscientific." Indeed, it is the uncritical application to economics of the methods of the natural sciences which is itself the unscientific procedure.

It is not surprising, therefore, to find that Austrians have for the most part eschewed empirical and statistical work. They have concentrated on deriving propositions of a *qualitative* rather than *quantitative* nature. These propositions follow from the basic insights into human nature referred to earlier, rather than from assumptions about the real-life content of preferences, knowledge, or expectations. For this reason, it is envisaged that such propositions will be true for *all* times and places rather than only for specific times and places.

The Appropriate Role of Empirical Work

In light of the Austrian reservations against empirical testing of economic theories, it seems appropriate to indicate two important roles that empirical work can and does play.

The first role concerns the status of the insights about human nature that Austrians use as basic assumptions. Mises liked to refer to them as a priori knowledge. But he did not suppose that such knowledge is completely and immediately made known to us

---

[32] Kirzner, "On the Method of Austrian Economics," in *Foundations of Modern Austrian Economics,* p. 43.

merely by introspection. At any time we undoubtedly fail to appreciate the nature and significance of certain features of the human personality, and interpret other features incorrectly. Moreover, yet other insights depend not only upon introspection but upon observation: The insight that man's preferences are unpredictable depends upon our *experience* that men *are* unpredictable in their actions. Similarly, the Austrian belief in a coordinating market process depends upon empirical assertions about how men learn from *experience.*

If this argument is correct, there is also an important role for empirical testing in the process of developing, modifying, and correcting economic theory itself. Empirical measurement and testing may suggest hitherto unnoticed flaws or omissions or undeveloped propositions in economic theory, and may help to resolve differences of opinion about such matters.

Mises, as we have remarked, thought of economic theory as limited to qualitative propositions that are true for all times and places. But the term "economic theory" is frequently used in a looser sense, to explain behavior in a particular country over a particular period of time. It has recently been observed, for example, that the analysis and prescriptions of Keynesian economics may have been appropriate in the time of Keynes but no longer are so, and similarly for the Phillips Curve.[33] The reason is that people learn from experience and react differently henceforth.

If economic theory is used in this more general sense, it clearly embodies assumptions about the beliefs held by people, and about the ways in which they respond to events. Whether these assumptions are correct is eminently a matter for empirical testing.

[33] J. Wiseman, "A Model of Inflation and the Government Deficit," in *The Dilemmas of Government Expenditure,* Institute of Economic Affairs Readings no. 15 (London, 1976), pp. 39-49; M. Friedman, *Inflation and Unemployment.*

III. Competition and the Market Process

Difficulties of "Perfect" Competition

If one had to identify a single concept at the heart of Austrian economics, it would undoubtedly be that of the market process. "Mainstream" economics is centered upon the notion of competitive equilibrium at a point in time characterized by perfect knowledge and coordinated plans on the part of the participants in the market. Austrians supplement (or even replace) this notion with that of a process taking place over time which is characterized not only by *lack* of knowledge and consequent *lack* of coordination, but also by *learning* and *increasing* coordination.[34]

Consider the conventional textbook analysis of perfect competition. Each consumer with given income chooses a basket of commodities at known prices to maximize his utility. Each producer chooses the bundle of inputs and outputs and the set of techniques which will maximize his profit, again at given prices. These prices are determined by aggregating the decisions of individual consumers and producers to generate total demand and supply curves for each industry. The intersection points of these curves determine equilibrium prices and quantities for all commodities. Everything happens very smoothly.

---

[34]Of course, the notion of competition as a process did not originate with the Austrians. It is to be found in Adam Smith and other classical writers. P. J. McNulty argues that only in this century has it been superseded by the static concept of perfect competition ("A Note on the History of Perfect Competition," *Journal of Political Economy,* August 1967).

Can such an analysis be reconciled with the real world, characterized as it is by lack of knowledge and by mistakes? To some extent it can. The conventional analyses of consumer and producer must be interpreted as referring to the *plans* of these individuals. The goods and techniques from which they choose are those of which they have knowledge at the time; the prices are those they expect to prevail when the time comes to buy or sell. The plans of these individuals are optimal for them in the light of their current views of the market.

These plans must now be put into effect. To the extent that they embody correct predictions about the environment and the actions of others, it will be possible to carry them out. But sooner or later a revision of plans will be desirable, either because of *errors* in forecasting or because *new opportunities* are noticed which had previously been missed. The decision-makers must, therefore, be represented as alert to their environment, in order that they may revise their plans when it seems to them advantageous to do so.

The concept of "economizing," or maximizing subject to *given* tastes and prices, is not adequate to encompass the search for *new* opportunities, whether new products or better terms for existing ones. Many Austrians reserve the term "entrepreneurship" to describe this latter power of alertness. The term "acting man" was coined by Mises to refer to the typical decision-maker equipped with the power not only to economize but also to exercise such entrepreneurship. Professor Kirzner emphasizes that "it is this entrepreneurial element that is responsible for our understanding of human action as active, creative, and human rather than as passive, automatic, and mechanical."[35]

Competition and the Market Process

According to the Austrian view, the key insight into competition is that different people know different things; the market process gathers and transmits these discrete and often contradictory bits

---

[35] I. M. Kirzner, *Competition and Entrepreneurship* (Chicago: University of Chicago Press, 1973), p. 35.

of information, thereby coordinating people's actions.[36] The importance of this idea is seen when examined in a little more detail.

In the context of the market, the term *entrepreneurship* refers to the alertness to profit opportunities not so far grasped by other market participants. In the simplest case, this response will consist of arbitrage: Where a commodity is unwittingly sold at different prices in different places or at different times, it is possible to profit by buying at the lowest prices and selling at the highest. In the more complex case, production may be seen as an opportunity to put together a bundle of inputs (labor, capital, etc.) costing less than the value of the output, or even yielding a different product which other firms have not yet noticed.

Thus profit is not necessarily (or even usually) the result of monopoly power. It is the result of successful entrepreneurial activity, the reward for noticing some lack of coordination in the market. Thus Professor Kirzner:

> The essence of the "profit incentive" (and in particular its significance for normative economics) is thus not to be seen as motivation to work harder or to allocate resources more efficiently. The profit incentive (including, of course, the disincentive of loss) operates most significantly by sparking the alertness of entrepreneurs—by encouraging them to keep their eyes open for new information that will lead to new plans.[37]

Especially in the British and American context, mention should be made of the subtle but pervasive and harmful effect that high marginal income taxes cannot fail to have on *entrepreneurial incentives.* There can be little incentive to be alert to opportunities the gain from which will accrue to unknown others decided by the government. Something of a vicious cycle may indeed be noticed. That over one-quarter of British Gross National Product is

---

[36]L. von Mises, *Human Action: A Treatise on Economics,* 3rd ed. rev. (Chicago: Henry Regnery, 1963); F. A. Hayek, "The Meaning of Competition" and other studies in his *Individualism and Economic Order* (Chicago: University of Chicago Press, 1948) and more recently "Competition as a Discovery Procedure," in his *New Studies in Philosophy, Politics, Economics and the History of Ideas* (Chicago: University of Chicago Press, 1978).

[37]Kirzner, *Competition and Entrepreneurship,* p. 223.

channeled *directly* through government is responsible for the high income-tax rates which sap the incentive to notice new opportunities—providing in turn fuel for the critics who point to the failure of the market to achieve prosperity, etc.

The very activity of exploiting opportunities brings them to the notice of other market participants, and they in turn respond by new alertness. Profits which previously existed because of unnoticed opportunities are now competed away. Whereas a variety of prices used to exist in the market, because sellers at one price were unaware that there were buyers at a higher price, over time a single price comes to rule as information is dispersed through the market. Thus, as Professor Kirzner explains:

> . . . even without changes in the basic data of the market (i.e., in consumer tastes, technological possibilities, and resource availabilities), the decisions made in one period of time generate systematic alterations in the corresponding decisions for the succeeding period. Taken over time, this series of systematic changes in the interconnected network of market decisions constitutes the market process.[38]

The situation depicted in the perfect competition model represents the situation when the competitive process has run its course. There are no further profit opportunities to be exploited; the market participants are fully coordinated. In such a situation there is no role for entrepreneurship. Mises saw the perfectly competitive model (or a variant of it, which he called the "evenly rotating economy") as serving a useful, albeit limited, function.

> In order to grasp the function of entrepreneurship and the meaning of profit and loss, we construct a system from which they are absent. . . . In eliminating the entrepreneur one eliminates the driving force of the whole system.[39]

Since, however, all action in the real world takes place in the face of more or less uncertainty, all action ipso facto contains an element of entrepreneurship.

Competition is thus seen as a device for *coordinating* the plans

---

[38] Ibid., p. 10.
[39] Mises, *Human Action,* pp. 248-9.

of market participants. To be sure, a piece of new information, or the intervention of a competitor, will disrupt someone's existing plan and force him to revise it. Many economists, including perhaps Schumpeter, see only this aspect of competition and thereby label it "disruptive" of equilibrium. But the very existence of unexploited profit opportunities which are seized by competitors is an indication that previous plans were somewhere not coordinated. By drawing attention to and remedying this lack of coordination, competition acts as an equilibrium force.

"Monopolistic" Competition

There have been several attempts to replace or supplement the notion of perfect competition. Most notable were the concepts of monopolistic and imperfect competition developed during the 1930s by, respectively, Professor E. H. Chamberlin of Harvard and Professor Joan Robinson of Cambridge, England.[40] According to Professor Kirzner, these attempts were completely on the wrong track:

> The authors of the new theory failed entirely to correctly identify the source of [the existing theory's] unrealistic character. Instead of attacking the equilibrium emphasis in the theory of pure competition, these authors introduced *different* equilibrium theories. . . . In the course of attempting to account for such market phenomena as product differentiation, advertising or markets in which few producers are to be found, the new theories were led to conclusions which grossly misinterpret the significance of these phenomena.[41]

Let us briefly examine the basis for this claim. The theory of monopolistic competition is generally believed to be more realistic than the previous theories of perfect competition and monopoly, because it allowed for product differentiation, advertising, and interdependent demand curves. Chamberlin's explanation of product differentiation, nevertheless, suffers from two deficien-

---

[40] E. H. Chamberlin, *The Theory of Monopolistic Competition,* 7th ed. (Cambridge: Harvard University Press, 1956); Joan Robinson, *The Economics of Imperfect Competition* (London: Macmillan, 1933).

[41] Kirzner, *Competition and Entrepreneurship,* p. 29.

cies. First, like the previous theories of perfect competition and monopoly, it assumes the demand curves to be somehow "given." There is no recognition of the need for manufacturers and consumers to *experiment* in order to find those products and variations which are most appropriate. Consequently, the theory of monopolistic competition rules out the possibility that a significant part of the product differentiation existing in the world today is not the result of a *final informed equilibrium choice* by consumers, but rather a reflection of a *continuing process of exploration.* Second, as others besides Austrians have pointed out,[42] the theory of monopolistic competition does not explain how product differentiation can persist in equilibrium—that is, why other firms cannot duplicate those varieties of product which turn out to be successful.

The Role of Advertising

Advertising represented something of an embarrassment to traditional economic theory. If consumers had perfect information about the products available, it was not clear what the role of advertising could be. It seemed to represent a waste of resources. But if consumers did not have perfect information, there would obviously be a need for its provision, and resources thus spent would not necessarily be wasted.

To Chamberlin and others, advertising was one way of conveying information to consumers about a product they knew existed. But to mix information with persuasion seemed undesirable, and the amount of resources devoted to advertising seemed excessive. Perhaps a more efficient and unbiased method of spreading the necessary information might be reports by independent consumer advisory units. Professor James E. Meade put this view:

> Of course, much advertisement of an informative nature is necessary and desirable. But much advertisement is not of this kind. A tax on advertisement would increase the incentive for firms to seek markets by cutting prices rather than by persuasive bamboozlement. . . .

[42]H. Demsetz, "The Notion of Equilibrium in Monopolistic Competition," *Journal of Political Economy,* February 1959, pp. 21-30.

Measures might be taken to replace much interested persuasive
advertisement with impartial information through the promotion
by the State of bodies for consumers' research and education.[43]

Austrian thinking provides a new insight into advertising. Consumers do *not* always know what products are available, and even
if they know of their existence, they are not always aware of their
properties. And consumers cannot, of course, seek further information about a product or property of whose existence they
are unaware. Consequently, there is an important role for the
manufacturer in bringing these new products to their notice. In
effect, he has to help the consumer to act entrepreneurially. For
this purpose, advertising may well have to be persuasive, even
accompanied by a catchy jingle, because it is necessary to attract
the consumer's attention, and persuade him that it will be worthwhile to take an interest.[44] Thus it is that Charles Atlas proclaims,
"You too can have a body like mine," because his potential customers are 98-pound weaklings who have given up hope.

Monopoly

Austrian views on markets with few producers—oligopoly— are
somewhat ambiguous and not treated at much length. It will
therefore be more fruitful to outline the Austrian position on
markets with a single producer—the case of monopoly.

It is traditionally assumed that a single producer will be able to
raise his price and thereby earn a monopoly profit, depending
upon the shape of his demand curve. It is not always explained
how he comes to know this demand curve, why he is a single
producer, and why entry (or the threat of it) of other firms does
not prevent him from acting as he does. For Austrians, these
questions are crucial.

---

[43] J. E. Meade, *The Intelligent Radical's Guide to Economic Policy* (London:
Allen and Unwin, 1975), pp. 49-50.
[44] Ralph Harris and Arthur Seldon, *Advertising in a Free Society* (London:
Institute of Economic Affairs, 1959) and *Advertising and the Public* (London:
Institute of Economic Affairs, 1962); Y. Brozen, *Advertising and Society* (New
York: New York University Press, 1974); I. M. Kirzner, "Advertising," in *The
Libertarian Alternative,* ed. T. R. Machan (Chicago: Nelson-Hall, 1974).

27

Demand curves are not somehow "given": They have to be discovered by experimenting, by trial and error. (Alchian and Allen use the term "price searcher."[45]) Even if a firm is a monopolist, it has to discover what its customers want and what they will pay for it. In other words, the presence of monopoly in no way obviates the need for the market process of discovery. In this sense the competitive character of the market process has not been affected. As Professor Kirzner puts it:

> The final equilibrium position toward which the market is tending may be drastically affected by monopoly resource ownership, but the process of bringing the decisions of market participants into more closely dovetailing patterns remains unchanged.[46]

Schumpeter always emphasized that the real source of competition, that which threatened a producer's very livelihood, arose not from other producers of the *same* product but from *new* and *better* products and techniques. Monopoly of the original product availed little against such attacks; hence the market was characterized by a "perennial gale of creative destruction."[47]

This approach leads in turn to the question of *why* a firm is a single seller of a given product. There are several possibilities. Other firms may not find it worthwhile to compete. I believe, for example, there is only one firm in Britain supplying academic gowns on loan for degree congregations, although others easily could. Such cases are no cause for concern.

Some firms may be protected from entry by the government. The British Post Office has a statutory monopoly of letters, telegraphs and telephones, though other firms would like to compete in various areas. Laker Airlines was for many years prevented by British and American governments from operating its cheap "Skytrain" to New York. Austrians have always condemned such special privileges.

Some firms may be producing products or varieties thereof which other firms have not seen as profitable, or whose potential

---

[45] Alchian and Allen, *University Economics.*

[46] Kirzner, *Competition and Entrepreneurship,* p. 21.

[47] J. A. Schumpeter, *Capitalism, Socialism and Democracy,* 3rd ed. (New York: Harper & Row, 1950).

profitability they have recognized only belatedly. Providing that competitors can enter, the monopoly position is then only temporary, and "monopoly profits" are more accurately described as "entrepreneurial profits," for they result from the successful exploitation of an opportunity which others have not yet seen. A pertinent example is provided by Xerox, which was bought by Rank Corporation after 40 other organizations had turned down the opportunity; yet in 1975 Rank Xerox achieved pretax profits of £184 million.[48]

Finally, a firm may be a monopolist because it owns the entire stock of some resource required to produce the products. Other firms would like to enter the market and are prevented from doing so not by the government but by the company itself. The monopolist is therefore able to restrict his output, increase his prices and earn true monopoly profits deriving from his monopoly ownership of the resource. Only in this last case does the market mechanism not ensure that resources are distributed according to the wishes of the consumers.[49]

The implications of monopoly for public policy are discussed in Chapter 5. It suffices here to establish the emphasis that Austrians place upon freedom of entry as a necessary and sufficient condition for competition in the sense of a market process.

Temporary Equilibrium Models

There has recently been a good deal of interest in mathematical models of temporary equilibrium, designed to incorporate uncertainty, information, and time into the static general equilibrium

---

[48] Monopolies and Mergers Commission, *Indirect Electrostatic Reprographic Equipment,* HC 47 (London: HMSO, December 1976).

[49] Mises, *Human Action.* However, other Austrians would disagree, taking the line that in practice a monopoly price can never be identified, or that the monopolist is himself a consumer. *See* M. N. Rothbard, *Man, Economy, and State,* chap. 10; W. Block, "Austrian Monopoly Theory: A Critique," *Journal of Libertarian Studies,* vol. 1 (1977), no. 4; D. T. Armentano, "A Critique of Neoclassical and Austrian Monopoly Theory," in *New Directions in Austrian Economics,* ed. L. M. Spadaro (Kansas City: Sheed Andrews and McMeel, 1978).

models of the last two decades.[50] It might appear that these models are consistent with the Austrian approach. I would maintain that a closer examination reveals a significant difference: They contain no element of alertness or entrepreneurship. Essentially, the agents are programmed with "expectation functions" and "decision functions" which enable them to operate in an environment of uncertainty and change. But though the specific forecasts made by the agents may change over time in response to changes in inputs, the "functions" themselves remain the same. Nothing will ever occur for which the agents are not prepared; nor can they ever initiate anything which was not preordained for them.[51]

The "Concentration Doctrine"

It is often suggested (usually in informal discussion between academics) that although the notion of a competitive process is helpful as an explanation of how competitive equilibrium is attained, nonetheless it is the theory of equilibrium which is more important. For all practical purposes the economy is "near enough" in equilibrium. In particular, it is said, this assumption is the most useful basis for empirical work.

It is therefore of interest to examine a group of studies which show that a theory of market process, in which the economy is explicitly assumed *not* to be in equilibrium but rather in *transition*, provides a quite different, and apparently superior, explanation of certain empirical data. Moreover, this alternative explanation based on a continuing market process has implications for government policy which are radically different from the implications of the theory based upon equilibrium.

The so-called "concentration doctrine" is the belief that collusion between firms is easier in industries where total output is

[50]F. H. Hahn, *On the Notion of Equilibrium in Economics* (Cambridge: At the University Press, 1973); J. M. Grandmont, "Temporary General Equilibrium Theory," *Econometrica,* April 1977, pp. 535-72.

[51]S. C. Littlechild, *Change Rules, O.K.?,* Inaugural Lecture delivered at the University of Birmingham, 28 May 1977, and published by the University.

concentrated in relatively few firms, and that collusion will, in turn, lead to higher prices and profits and lower output. This doctrine is frequently put forward to justify policies of merger control and even forcible deconcentration.[52]

If this theory is correct, we should observe higher profit ratios in highly concentrated industries. The evidence is not entirely convincing. An important pioneering study, by Professor Joe S. Bain, was based on data for 42 U.S. industries over the period 1936-40.[53] He found that in the group of highly concentrated industries, where the eight largest firms accounted for 70 percent or more of value added, the average profit rate was significantly higher than in the less concentrated industries.

This study has been examined by Professor Yale Brozen of the University of Chicago. He showed that even if concentration had facilitated collusion in 1940, it had not been possible to keep out new entry for a long period: Fifteen years later the high- and low-profit rates in Bain's industries had moved back toward the average.[54]

Professor Harold Demsetz analyzed the same problem from a different point of view.[55] If concentration facilitates collusion, not only the large firms but also the small firms in a concentrated industry would benefit from higher prices and would show higher profit rates. Yet the evidence he adduced did not show that profit rates of small firms increased with concentration. Demsetz also suggested that those firms tended to grow fastest which noticed and exploited profitable opportunities sooner than others. An industry would be more highly concentrated the wider the difference in ability between its constituent firms. Higher concentration should therefore imply a wider difference in profit rates

[52] H. Demsetz, *The Market Concentration Doctrine,* AEI-Hoover Policy Study no. 7 (Washington, D.C.: American Enterprise Institute, 1973).

[53] J. S. Bain, "Relation of Profit Rate to Industry Concentration: American Manufacturing 1936-40," *Quarterly Journal of Economics* 65 (1951): 293-324.

[54] Y. Brozen, "The Antitrust-Task Force Deconcentration Recommendation," *Journal of Law and Economics,* October 1970. His later work showed that Bain's results were biased by a statistical error resulting from the incorrect assumption that industries were in long-run equilibrium: Y. Brozen, "Bain's Concentration and Rates of Return Revisited," *Journal of Law and Economics,* October 1971.

[55] H. Demsetz, "Industry Structure, Market Rivalry and Public Policy," *Journal of Law and Economics,* April 1973.

between small and large firms. The evidence collected by Demsetz supported this hypothesis.

These results seem to reject the theory that concentration allows collusion which, in turn, leads to higher profit rates. Rather, variations in profit rates are to be explained by differences in the perception of, and speed of reaction to, *changes* in the underlying market phenomena. These changes set in motion a market process which takes time to work out; indeed, firms are *always* in transition. Some have learned and grown, some are learning and growing, others have misjudged the situation and are shrinking. The profits achieved by these firms reflect their success in adapting themselves to the changing conditions of the market. In short, we have here an apposite illustration of the Austrian approach to competition as a process. This theory, which implies the ever changing structure of industry, seems more successful than the "concentration doctrine" in explaining the relationship between profit, size of firm, and concentration.

The competitive process theory has quite different policy implications from those of the concentration doctrine. To break up firms or to prohibit mergers in order to deconcentrate the industry is not likely to decrease profit rates. On the contrary, it is more likely in the short run to force firms to operate at inefficient sizes with the result that prices will be higher than they otherwise would be, and in the long run to discourage firms from noticing and exploiting opportunities to reduce costs or introduce new products. These and related issues will be further developed in Chapter 5.

IV. The Role of Government

The Mixed Economy

The appropriate role of government is the subject matter of "welfare economics." In essence, it is argued that under specified "ideal" conditions, a competitive economy will bring about an allocation of resources that is "efficient." But these conditions may not be met in the real world, and so there may be cases of "market failure." The job of the welfare economist is to identify such failures and to prescribe appropriate government policy for dealing with them.

This kind of thinking is frequently used to explain and defend the "mixed economy" that characterizes almost all non-Communist countries today. A distinguished proponent of this view is Professor James E. Meade of Cambridge University. His book, *The Intelligent Radical's Guide to Economic Policy: The Mixed Economy*, develops his argument, from which it will be convenient to quote at some length.

The "intelligent radical" is concerned to encourage efficiency, security, and participation; above all, however, he dislikes large concentrations of power, which threaten independence, and large concentrations of wealth, which perpetuate class distinctions. From these value judgments the following conclusions for policy are derived:

> The intelligent radical . . . starts by advocating the removal of all unnecessary restrictions on the operation of free competitive markets. But he recognizes that on the foundation of this market mechanism there must be built a super-structure of governmental interventions and controls. Some of these interventions are needed simply to set a background of conditions in which free competition can work effectively; others are needed to replace entirely the mechanism of competitive markets, where that mechanism

33

cannot be expected to operate effectively; others have an inter-mediate purpose, namely to modify without replacing the opera-tion of a market price mechanism. . . .

First, the intelligent radical . . . will realize how essential . . . it is to his purpose to control inflations and deflations. . . .

Second, . . . government intervention is needed to submit to appropriate social controls the use of the monopolistic powers of large corporate concerns, whether these can be huge conglomer-ate industrial concerns or powerful labour monopolies.

Third, in some cases economies of large scale are so important that monopoly is inevitable, as in the case of railway transport, the generation and distribution of electricity, and such like ser-vices. In these cases, the intelligent radical will advocate outright state ownership and control.

Fourth, there are many goods and services—such as the admin-istration of justice and maintenance of law and order—which in the nature of things cannot be purchased separately by each indi-vidual for his own separate enjoyment, but which must be pur-chased and enjoyed in common by all members of the community. The intelligent radical will recognise the fact that in modern con-ditions the central and local governments must play a large role in the provision of such public goods.

Fifth, the intelligent radical . . . advocates State action to pro-mote equality of opportunity [and] . . . far-reaching direct fiscal measures should be taken by budgetary taxes and expenditures to moderate the high, and to supplement the low, incomes and properties.

Sixth, the intelligent radical realises that the market mechanism cannot be expected to deal adequately with planning for the un-certainties of the future, and that its operation may well be aided by some measure of governmental indicative planning.

Seventh, he also recognises the need for the central planning of large structural changes in the economy.

Finally, he recognises the need for controls and interventions in order to cope with important cases in which the market mech-anism will otherwise neglect to take into account important items of social, as opposed to private, costs and benefits. Problems of environmental control, of the use of exhaustible resources, and of population growth will on these grounds be recognised as raising issues which call for governmental action.[56]

Meade is here expressing a view held by many, if not most, economists and, indeed, perhaps intuitively, by members of the general public. His argument is clear and concise, and his initial value-judgments will surely command widespread sympathy. In

[56]Meade, *Intelligent Radical's Guide,* pp. 13-16.

his vigorous defense of competition, he will certainly have the support of Austrians. Nevertheless there are many other aspects of his proposals which raise serious doubts about the desirability of the mixed economy.

Austrian Skepticism about "Welfare Economics"

To begin with, it is clear, in the light of the principles sketched out in Chapters 2 and 3, that an Austrian is necessarily skeptical about the "welfare economics" lying behind these policies. He has reservations in three major respects.

First, he cannot accept the implied description of how the market mechanism operates. He sees hardly any reference in welfare economics to uncertainty and mistakes. He finds competition presented as a state of equilibrium with *given* commodities and techniques, rather than as a dynamic process of *searching* for *new* commodities and *better* techniques. He finds more concern with achieving the "efficient" set of prices and outputs than with ensuring a steady reduction in prices and increase in outputs. (This proposition has been discussed at some length in the preceding chapter.)

Second, the Austrian finds no detailed explanation in welfare economics of how government is supposed to obtain the information necessary to carry out its assigned tasks. The knowledge required for a general assessment is not to be found collected in one place, but rather dispersed throughout the many members of the economy. Moreover, the relevant knowledge does not for the most part refer to "facts" about the past but to preferences and opportunities in the future, which exist only in people's heads and are therefore highly subjective. This proposition will become clear in the succeeding chapters.[57]

[57]L. von Mises, "Economic Calculation in a Socialist Community," in *Collectivist Economic Planning,* ed. F. A. Hayek (Fairfield, N.J.: Kelley, 1935); F. A. Hayek, "The Use of Knowledge in Society," and "Socialist Calculation I, II, III," in his *Individualism and Economic Order;* M. N. Rothbard, "Toward a Reconstruction of Utility and Welfare Economics," in *On Freedom and Free Enterprise,* ed. M. Sennholz (Princeton: Van Nostrand, 1956).

Third, as Menger and Hayek have pointed out, institutions for solving social problems may in principle be of two kinds: pragmatic (reflecting conscious design) or organic (arising unintentionally). It is necessary to choose an appropriate balance between the two kinds of institutions, to choose an appropriate pragmatic framework of regulations and government policies within which organic processes can operate. To Austrians, welfare economics fails sufficiently to appreciate the nature, resilience, and power of organic processes, and hence tends to see the solution as necessarily pragmatic, requiring a government organization to exert conscious control.

Austrians have not been alone in this conclusion. In particular, the authors mentioned in Chapter 1, especially Demsetz, have emphasized that our interpretation and evaluation of the market and government depend crucially upon the availability (or otherwise) of information.[58]

In recent years there has also been considerable important work on the economics of government behavior. I have in mind here the theories of property rights, public choice (or economics of politics), and economic regulations.[59] These three somewhat different approaches have in common that they focus on the nature of the choices facing individuals, whether as producers, consumers, employees, taxpayers, voters, civil servants, politicians, etc. They explore the kinds of opportunities open to these individuals, and the ways in which pressures of various kinds affect their evaluation of the outcomes of choices. Considerable insights have thereby been obtained into the reasons for, and working of,

---

[58] H. Demsetz, "Information and Efficiency: Another Viewpoint."

[59] A. A. Alchian and R. A. Kessel, "Competition, Monopoly and the Pursuit of Money in Universities," in National Bureau of Economic Research, *Aspects of Labor* (New York, 1962); Alchian and Allen, *University Economics;* Buchanan and Tullock, *Calculus of Consent;* J. M. Buchanan, *The Inconsistencies of the National Health Service,* Institute of Economic Affairs Occasional Paper no. 7 (London, 1965); G. Tullock, *The Vote Motive,* Institute of Economic Affairs Hobart Paperback no. 9 (London, 1976); W. A. Niskanen, *Bureaucracy: Servant or Master?,* Institute of Economic Affairs Hobart Paperback no. 5 (London, 1973); G. J. Stigler, "The Theory of Economic Regulation," *Bell Journal of Economics and Management Science,* Spring 1971, pp. 3-21; L. de Alessi, "An Economic Analysis of Government Ownership and Regulation," *Public Choice,* Fall 1974.

government policies and organizations, ranging from the National Health Service to the regulation of the professions.

This work is an example of the further application of the principle of methodological individualism. As such, it seems to me nicely to complement the Austrian approach. Indeed, it seems to lead to similar implications for public policy. Nonetheless, though it runs parallel to the Austrian approach, it is not the approach which Austrians themselves have used.[60] For this reason, since the theme of this discussion is the Austrians, I shall occasionally refer to public choice and property rights but will not emphasize their significance as much as their importance otherwise warrants.

Is There an Austrian View on the Role of Government?

While it is true that, for the reasons just given, Austrians would not accept most of the arguments of welfare economics, it is by no means clear that they share a common view about the policy implications of economic theory.

Austrians are nowadays associated with the free market, and Lachmann has indeed described the Austrians as "defenders of the market economy." To some extent, this position reflects the influence of Mises and Hayek, who were both strong liberals (in the 19th-century sense), though Menger and Böhm-Bawerk probably held similar views. Yet this was not always so. Wieser and Schumpeter envisaged a relatively extensive role for government. At the other extreme, there is nowadays a libertarian/no-government element in the Austrian camp, headed by Rothbard, which agrees that economic theory does not imply any particular role for the state.

The writers listed as apparently sympathetic to the Austrian approach seem to fall into two groups. Some are clearly identified with a free-market position. For others, it is quite impossible to tell from their writings (or indeed from casual personal acquaintance) where their political sympathies lie.

---

[60]But cf. M. N. Rothbard, *Power and Market: Government and the Economy,* 2nd ed. (Kansas City: Sheed Andrews and McMeel, 1977). Cf also, F. A. Hayek, "Economic Freedom and Representative Government," in his *New Studies in Philosophy.*

The contribution of Austrian economic theory to the understanding of how economies work is independent of the philosophical positions of Austrian economists. At present, it is true that most Austrians place a high value on individual freedom and would probably support the market economy for that reason alone. However, if an economist held certain value-judgments—for example, that private property is immoral, or that (economic) power tends to corrupt, or that working for profit is degrading—he could perfectly well advocate a very substantial role for government, or at least severe limitations on private enterprise, while fully accepting Austrian economic theory.

The important question for policy remains: How far would the "intelligent radical" who starts with the kind of value judgments Meade has assumed, and who accepts the superiority of Austrian economic theory over conventional welfare economics, still favor the kind of "mixed economy" Meade has proposed?

It may be helpful to indicate in advance the view held by Mises, as interpreted by Kirzner:

> . . . when one examines Mises's many statements about economic policy, whether they be about price controls, tariffs, antitrust policy, or anything else, one invariably discovers that his conclusions do not at all reflect his own personal valuations. They reflect only his opinions concerning the degree of success with which others are pursuing *their* purposes. . . .
>
> This was made very clear indeed in Mises's oral presentations. He would emphasize again and again that interventionist policies are "wrong," not from the point of view of the economist himself, but from the point of view of those initiating these policies (or at least from the point of view of those whose well-being the policies are supposed to enhance).[61]

Mises would not deny that the various measures of a mixed economy benefit particular interest-groups in the short run. But in the long run he thought all would be made worse off.

---

[61]I. M. Kirzner, "Philosophical and Ethical Implications of Austrian Economics," in *Foundations of Modern Austrian Economics,* p. 82.

V. Policy on Competition

The "Mainstream" View

A small country like Britain inevitably faces the dilemma that if firms are allowed to exploit the advantages of economies of scale, they may grow so large that there is a danger of monopoly, or at least collusion among the few firms in the industry. The "man in the street" has probably been most concerned about monopoly insofar as there is a presumed transfer of wealth from consumers to producers in the form of high profits. Economists have traditionally eschewed this distributive aspect and objected to monopoly on the ground that it prevents the efficient allocation of resources associated with perfect competition. But everyone seems to agree that, since monopolists will restrict output to raise prices and profits, it is necessary to prevent (a) the exploitation of monopoly power, (b) the creation of monopoly power in the first place, and (c) collusive practices among otherwise competitive firms.[62]

Policy on competition in Britain today seems to reflect these views. It has three major elements:

1. The Monopolies and Mergers Commission may be asked to investigate whether the "things done" by large firms, and proposed mergers, may be expected to operate against the public interest. If so, government has power to prohibit such activities or mergers.

---

[62]Cf. the recent statement by Roy Hattersley, the Prices Secretary, to a meeting of West Midlands businessmen: "When Government is inactive, monopolies develop, mergers are made, agreements in restraint of trade are signed. So I hope you will agree that the achievement of your aim of greater competition involves Government action" (*Birmingham Post,* 11 March 1978).

2. A broad range of agreements between firms must be publicly registered and may be brought before the Restrictive Trade Practices Court, where they will be held illegal unless the firms can satisfy the Court that the agreements are in the "public interest."
3. "Emergency" measures of price control have been in force over the past few years, whereby price increases for all but the smallest firms are thoroughly evaluated by the Price Commission and are allowed only on specific grounds.

Some economists have doubted whether the distortion caused by monopoly is very severe. In 1954, Professor Arnold C. Harberger of Chicago University made rough calculations which suggested that the net value of output lost due to monopoly in U.S. industry amounted at most to 0.1 percent of GNP.[63] Subsequent authors, on different assumptions, have argued for percentages as high as 5 percent, but these calculations still leave some doubt whether monopoly (excluding "natural monopoly") is worth bothering about.

On the other hand, it has recently been noted that in order to attain a monopoly position, firms will find it worthwhile to incur expenditure up to the level of prospective monopoly profit. This has led Professors Keith Cowling and Denis Mueller, of the Universities of Warwick and Maryland respectively, to argue that

> . . . the "monopoly problem" is broader than traditionally suggested. A large part of this problem lies not in the height of monopoly prices and profits *per se*, but in the resources wasted in their creation and protection.[64]

They calculate that in the year 1968-69, losses due to monopoly power of the top 102 U.K. firms amounted to between £970 million and £1400 million (depending upon the method of calculation). This represents 9 to 13 percent of gross corporate profits. The authors therefore call for intensified enforcement of antitrust policy, beginning with the largest firms such as British Petroleum and Shell, which (according to their estimates) together

[63] A. C. Harberger, "Monopoly and Resource Allocation," *American Economic Review,* May 1954, pp. 73-87.
[64] K. Cowling and D. C. Mueller, "The Social Costs of Monopoly Power," *Economic Journal,* December 1978, pp. 727-48.

accounted for a monopoly cost of up to £285 million in the same year.

An Alternative Interpretation of Profit

Austrians, as we have seen, have not viewed monopoly in the same light as welfare economists. Neither the number of firms in an industry nor the rate of profits earned is, in itself, a cause for alarm. On the contrary, insofar as profits reflect successful entrepreneurial awareness, they are a measure of consumer satisfaction, an indication that some coordination has been achieved where none existed before. It was in this light that we interpreted the £184 million profits earned by Rank Xerox.

Now these profits were no doubt achieved by setting such a high price that the volume of photocopying was restricted below its "competitive" size. On the other hand, had it not been for the lure of this temporary monopoly profit, the arrival of photocopying in Britain might have been delayed for several years, presumably at very considerable loss to both producers and the general public.

In other words, the appropriate comparison is not between an existing product supplied at a high price and that same product supplied at a low price. It is between a product supplied at a high price and *no product at all!* It is this insight which provides a counter to the argument of Professors Cowling and Mueller. Even if resources *are* used up in an attempt to achieve a monopoly position, nonetheless that may be a price worth paying if the result is to make a product available sooner than it otherwise would be.

The distinctive Austrian approach is further illustrated by the British Monopolies and Mergers Commission's condemnation of Hoffman-La Roche for making excessive profits from the sale of the tranquilizers Librium and Valium.[65] The company agreed to

---

[65] Monopolies and Mergers Commission, *Report on Supply of Chlordiazepoxide and Diazepam,* HC 197 (London: HMSO, April 1973). A critical study of this and other Monopolies Commission reports may be found in George Polanyi, *Which Way Monopoly Policy?,* Institute of Economic Affairs Research Monograph no. 30 (London, 1973).

repay a not inconsiderable sum to the National Health Service and to lower the prices of the two drugs henceforth. The utilization of these drugs will thereby increase, to the benefit of existing patients and those within whose price range these drugs now fall for the first time. Seen from a short-run point of view, this action by the government has improved the allocation of resources by relaxing the monopoly restriction on output.

From a longer-run point of view, the issue is not so clear-cut. If it becomes common practice to control drug prices, will pharmaceutical companies risk the heavy expense of basic research necessary to produce new drugs? Allegedly, fewer than one in every 200 compounds proves successful. The danger is that limiting monopoly profits may remove the incentives to exploit opportunities of mutual benefit to producers and consumers, or at least delay the date at which new ideas come to light.

The Role of Patents in Monopoly

Rank Xerox and Hoffman-La Roche do, however, highlight a different cause of concern to Austrians. Presumably one of the reasons for the high level of profits, and for the lack of actively competing firms, is the existence of patents. Other firms would like to compete but are not allowed to do so. It is here that Austrians would probably see the solution to such "monopoly problem" as exists.

The purpose of a patent is to encourage innovation in pursuit of monopoly profit. The danger lies in the restriction of entry consequent upon conferring this special property right. It may be true that without the protection of a patent, less money would be spent on research and development in hitherto protected areas, and innovation there might be reduced. On the other hand, resources used there have an opportunity cost: They would otherwise be used in other directions. Research and innovation would by no means cease altogether, for there is still a gain (a temporary monopoly profit) to be made from being first in the field. Moreover, abolishing patent protection would encourage the early exploitation and improvement by competitors of those innovations made by others.

The above case for the abolition of patents has been argued by the late Professor Sir Arnold Plant, and most Austrians would probably subscribe to it.[66] Austrians must therefore view with concern the recent extension in Britain of the duration of patents from 16 to 20 years and the proposed introduction of licensing for photocopying.[67] The experience of Italy, which has only a very limited patent system, deserves further study.

Since Austrians place their faith in entrepreneurial profits resulting from such temporary monopoly positions, they must be even more concerned about a recent legal judgment in New York. It was held that Kodak had violated the antitrust laws and monopolized the market in amateur cameras, color print paper, and film. The reason was that Kodak had failed to give its competitors early warning of its decision to introduce new films and cameras with enough information that its competitors could be in a position to offer alternative products.[68]

Mergers and Restrictive Practices

Policy on mergers follows naturally from policy on monopoly. If a single firm in an industry is not undesirable per se, nor is a merger to create one. Indeed, merging is one obvious way of competing. To prevent mergers is to protect other firms from competition, perhaps to prevent the adoption of some new technique or mode of organization and thereby to impede the competitive process.

Many economists have argued that the potential advantages of mergers resulting from economies of scale should be estimated and compared to the potential disadvantages from higher prices. In Britain the Monopolies and Mergers Commission is now

---

[66] A. Plant, "The Economic Theory Concerning Patents for Inventions," *Economica,* February 1934; Rothbard, *Man, Economy, and State,* chap. 10. Mises, however, did not commit himself; *see* his *Human Action,* pp. 661-2.

[67] The extension of patent protection was enacted by the Patents Act, 1977; the correspondence on the photocopying proposals in the *Times* (London) culminated in an editorial, "The Flood of Facsimiles," on 24 January 1978.

[68] *New York Times,* 26 February 1978 (article by K. I. Clearwaters).

required to do this only if the likely disadvantages seem serious. In the light of recent studies on the (lack of) profitability of mergers, however, the British Secretary of State for Prices and Consumer Protection is currently being urged to adopt a "stiffer" policy on competition involving the prohibition of mergers "where real benefits cannot be proved."[69]

The difficulty with this new proposal (indeed, with the present arrangement also) is that information about the past is difficult to obtain and predictions about the future are notoriously unreliable. This difficulty had led to suggestions that merger appraisals by the Commission might usefully be replaced by prohibitions on undesirable conduct after the event. Such prohibitions would be enforceable through the Courts.[70] Moreover, future competition will often come, as Schumpeter stressed, from quite unexpected sources. It is not surprising, therefore, that the Monopolies and Mergers Commission has been criticized for underestimating the strength of competition, and, therefore, biasing its judgments against mergers.[71]

Restrictive Practices: A Dilemma for Austrians

Restrictive practices pose a dilemma. On the one hand, many practices such as exclusive dealing between manufacturers and suppliers or distributors are undoubtedly intended to prevent new entry. They thereby impede the competitive process, and it would seem that current laws against them might be strengthened. On the other hand, it may be argued that this is their very merit. Protection from competition provides an inducement to make large and risky investments that otherwise would not be made.[72]

[69] *Times* (London), "Business Diary," 4 January 1978. The studies referred to presumably include G. Meeks, *Disappointing Marriage: A Study of the Gains from Merger,* University of Cambridge, Department of Applied Economics Occasional Paper no. 51 (Cambridge: At the University Press, 1977).

[70] M. E. Beesley, "Mergers and Economic Welfare," in *Mergers, Takeovers and the Structure of Industry,* Institute of Economic Affairs Readings no. 10 (London, 1973).

[71] C. K. Rowley, "Mergers and Public Policy in Great Britain," *Journal of Law and Economics,* April 1968, pp. 75-132.

[72] Schumpeter, *History of Economic Analysis;* Richardson, *Information and Investment.*

On balance, most Austrians would probably not favor laws against restrictive practices, relying for protection once again on the possibility that new entry would overcome such barriers.

In this connection, it may be observed that restrictive practices in several industries seem to stem from a government-granted monopoly position, notably the professions such as accounting, law, medicine, and architecture. Austrians would therefore be unwilling to grant such a privileged status to those occupations like hairdressing and insurance brokerage, which are currently applying for official recognition in Britain.[73]

The British Monopolies and Mergers Commission and the Price Commission suffer a further disadvantage to which the principle of methodological individualism should alert us. Since the government is involved in initiating and/or implementing the work of these commissions, a *political* element will inevitably emerge. Takeovers are occasionally referred to the Commission in response to pressure from people likely to lose jobs, and investigations that might prove embarrassing are not always authorized. Nor has government always found it convenient to implement the recommendations of the Commission. Such behavior by government must be expected: A government must be expected to respond to political pressures as it perceives them, and whatever instrument is most convenient will inevitably be used.

The Restrictive Trade Practices Court, being part of the British legal system, is essentially immune from this disadvantage (though of course the scope of the legislation is a matter of government policy, and presumably it is not thought politically expedient to bring unions and nationalized industries within it). It is arguable, however, that if this Court is continued, the opportunity to prosecute should be extended to those adversely affected by restrictive practices, who have most incentive to discover the practices and provide the necessary information.[74]

---

[73] *Times* (London) 3 November 1976 and 25 January 1978, respectively.
[74] Beesley, "Mergers and Economic Welfare."

VI. Controlling Britain's Nationalized Industries

The Situation Today

In various industries, it is alleged, the economies of large-scale production are so great that it would be inefficient to have more than one producer. It would be impractical and undesirable, Meade argued, to impose a permanent system of price control on such "natural monopolies":

> The second and final solution is the social ownership and management of the activities concerned. Railways, roads, gas, electricity, sewage, water supply, telephones are all examples where price competition in a free market is out of the question.[75]

In 1975, the nationalized industries accounted for more than a tenth of Britain's national product and nearly a fifth of total fixed investment. These proportions have subsequently increased with the nationalization of the aircraft and shipbuilding industries, and the acquisition of British Leyland and other companies.

On what principles should the nationalized industries be operated? Meade argues that "a socialized concern should take into account all the social costs involved" and that "prices should be set equal to marginal costs, even though this may mean running the nationalized concern at an abnormally high profit or running it at a loss." These ideas reflect traditional welfare economics. Under competition there is a tendency for price to be forced down to the level of marginal cost (the cost of a small addition to output), and for investments to be undertaken if and only if they promise to earn a return in excess of the cost of capital. In this way, the

[75]Meade, *Intelligent Radical's Guide,* p. 51.

welfare economist argues, perfect competition leads to an efficient allocation of resources. Consequently, where competition is nonexistent, the nationalized industry should act *as if* it were in a perfectly competitive situation. Unlike many proponents of nationalization, however, Meade urges that "nationalized concerns should not be protected from direct or indirect competition from outside sources."

The first British nationalized industries were typically required only to produce efficiently, to meet demand, and to break even. The more precise instructions in the 1967 White Paper[76] represented a modest victory for the advocates of welfare economics. "In addition to recovering accounting costs," it said, "prices need to be reasonably related to costs at the margin." The White Paper also required investment proposals to be expressed in present values by the use of a specified test rate of discount (8 percent, later raised to 10 percent), urged the nationalized industries to look for ways of economizing on manpower, and laid down for each industry a financial objective to act as an incentive to management and as a standard of performance.

It cannot be claimed that the 1967 White Paper has been an outstanding success. On the contrary, the recent report by Britain's National Economic Development Office was extremely critical of the current framework of control.

> . . . there are certain features of the relationship between government and nationalised industries which came through so clearly in our inquiry that we believe they can be stated without risk of contradiction:
> — there is a lack of trust and mutual understanding between those who run the nationalised industries and those in government (politicians and civil servants) who are concerned with their affairs;
> — there is confusion about the respective roles of the boards of nationalised industries, Ministers and Parliament, with the result that accountability is seriously blurred;
> — there is no systematic framework for reaching agreement on long-term objectives and strategy, and no assurance of continuity when decisions are reached;

[76] *Nationalised Industries: A Review of Financial and Economic Objectives,* Cmnd. 3437 (London: HMSO, 1967), p. 8.

> — there is no effective system for measuring the performance
> of nationalised industries and assessing managerial com-
> petence.[77]

Why has the framework proposed by the 1967 White Paper been so unsuccessful? The explanation is twofold. In the first place, the *intellectual* task facing the nationalized industries was misunderstood, and the rules derived from static welfare economics were inappropriate to the real world of uncertainty in which the industries operate. In the second place, the White Paper failed to take account of the *political* context of the nationalized industries, the reasons for their initial nationalization, and the political pressures bearing on them.

The first of these aspects was analyzed by Mises and Hayek in the course of the debate on socialist planning.[78] Their ideas were developed by the British subjectivists G. F. Thirlby and Jack Wiseman.[79] The second aspect has been dealt with most recently, mainly in the U.S. context, by the writers on public choice, property rights, and economic regulation, to whom we referred earlier.[80]

Inappropriate Rules

The pricing and investment rules prescribed by the White Paper are derived from the familiar model of static general equilibrium. They presume that the relevant products, demands, resources, resource prices, and techniques are "given," so that the task of the manager in a nationalized industry is merely to calculate the cheapest way of supplying demand and to price accordingly. In

---

[77]*A Study of UK Nationalised Industries* (London: HMSO, 1976), p. 8.

[78]Mises, "Economic Calculation in a Socialist Community"; Hayek, "The Use of Knowledge in Society" and "Socialist Calculation I, II, III"; Rothbard, "Toward a Reconstruction of Utility and Welfare Economics." *See also* Rothbard, *Man, Economy, and State,* p. 824.

[79]For example, G. F. Thirlby, "Economists' Cost Rules and Equilibrium Theory," *Economica,* May 1960; J. Wiseman, "The Theory of Public Utility Price — An Empty Box," *Oxford Economic Papers* 9 (1957): 56-74. These papers are reprinted with others in Buchanan and Thirlby, *L.S.E. Essays on Cost.*

[80]*See* n. 59 above.

49

such an environment, cost is "objective" because it is merely the sum of the known prices of known inputs, and it may easily be verified whether or not the industry is setting price equal to marginal cost.

In practice, these data are not "given." The task of the manager is precisely *to find out what they are*: to discover what products consumers want, what resources and techniques are available, and what prices are likely to have to be paid. The market mechanism, as we have seen, is a process of conjecture and experiment. It continuously reallocates resources to new uses which seem preferable to previous uses, and which earlier had perhaps not even been imagined.

It follows that the relevant cost of production, whether marginal, average, or total, is not objective but *subjective*: It is not the money outlay but the value of output in some alternative foregone use, and this alternative use is not "given" but exists only in the mind of the manager(s). Two managers with different knowledge about available alternatives, or different views about the future, will associate different costs with the very same output. Since the correctness of beliefs about the future cannot be established objectively (at the time), neither manager can be said to be wrong—each is right, given his beliefs.

Two conclusions follow. First, since it is impossible to check a manager's beliefs, it is impossible to check whether prices are being "reasonably related to costs at the margin," that is, whether the prescribed policy is being carried out. Second, even if a manager were correctly following his instructions, it does not necessarily mean that he will be successful in discovering new consumer demands and the best ways of meeting them.

Exactly analogous difficulties apply to the test rate of discount which is prescribed for assessing investment proposals. It is impossible to tell whether a manager really believes the estimates of revenue that support his case, and even if he does, he is not necessarily correct, nor does this preclude him from overlooking yet more favorable opportunities.

Private firms have similar difficulties in monitoring the performance of their employees and subsidiaries, but the important difference is that the market provides an essential "feedback."

Entrepreneurs who are successful in discovering and meeting the wishes of consumers are rewarded by profits; those who are unsuccessful are penalized by losses. The "feedback" provides an incentive to good performance and at the same time redistributes resources to people who appear most competent in using them. Finally, the possibility of competition means that a failure to exploit an opportunity by one firm is likely to be remedied by another. In this way, competition facilitates the task of owners of resources and safeguards the interests of consumers.

Neither of these benefits—"feedback" and competition—is available in the nationalized industries. They are almost always statutory monopolies, so that new entry by firms with superior ideas is precluded. Cross-subsidization of loss-making activities by monopoly profits is quite normal, the pattern of prices and products is subject to political pressures, and quite frequently losses are borne out of general taxation. Thus the suppression of competition makes it exceedingly difficult to know which activities ought to be encouraged, which industries ought to be expanded, and which managers ought to be promoted.

In sum, it is impossible to tell whether the prescribed rules for pricing and investment by nationalized industries are being followed, and if they are it does not guarantee that the best pattern of resource allocation is being achieved. The task is to find this best pattern, which moreover is constantly changing over time. Nationalization invariably removes a vital part of the information "feedback" and protection generated by the free-market mechanism.

Motivation and Political Pressures

It is commonly believed that industries are nationalized in order to protect consumers from exploitation by a natural monopoly. An examination of the history of these industries soon reveals this belief to be a myth. Telegraphs were nationalized in Britain in order to protect government revenues deriving from the postal monopoly, and telephones in turn were nationalized to protect government revenues deriving from the telegraph monopoly.

51

Municipal water companies were set up to provide service where private companies had not yet found it profitable to do so, and private companies were later regulated and nationalized in order to facilitate the cross-subsidization of consumers. Competing steel companies were nationalized in order to control the "commanding heights" of the economy. The recent nationalization of the aircraft and shipbuilding industries has clearly been provoked by the desire to protect existing jobs.

It is equally fallacious to believe that industries, once nationalized, are operated with the prime aim of securing the efficient allocation of resources. Nationalization has protected coal miners and postal workers from faster rates of closure, as it has protected suppliers to the electricity industry and the Post Office from falling demand.

Furthermore, in the last few years, government instructions to the nationalized industries have alternated between "standstills" on prices and investment so as to combat inflation and exhortations to raise prices so as to break even or to accelerate investment in order to avoid unemployment. These instructions have made it clear that the microeconomic principles of the White Paper designed to promote long-run efficient resource allocation are clearly subordinate to the day-to-day requirements of macroeconomic policy and demand management. The principles set out in the 1967 White Paper are at best an irrelevance, and at worst a hindrance, to the attempts of both government and nationalized industries to create or protect jobs, redistribute income, fight inflation, or stimulate the economy.

An Alternative Framework

We can now see why the framework provided by the 1967 White Paper was bound to fail. In the first place, it constructed a set of rules derived from the inadequate theoretical basis of static equilibrium, which was useless in the real world of imperfect knowledge. In the second place, the framework erroneously assumed a widespread and overwhelming desire to seek efficient resource allocation, which in practice was not the relevant assumption to make. In short, the White Paper foundered because it neglected the implications of the twin principles of methodological individualism and subjectivism.

Let us assume for the moment that a government has inherited a set of nationalized industries and wishes to promote the efficient allocation of resources. What kind of framework is indicated? Four principles suggest themselves:

1. The managers of the industries must be given incentives to seek out and meet the demands of consumers, they must be rewarded for doing so, and the selection of top managers and the allocation of funds should reflect this success. In practice, net revenue (possibly in relation to a target) is the most effective criterion of serving the market. Stronger incentives to managers could be provided by bonuses linked to the industry's financial performance.[81] A higher proportion of self-finance, which offers the industry the attraction of wider latitude in using its profits, is also an incentive to earn the profits in the first place. At the same time, if the borrowing rate for capital from the British National Loans Fund were raised to the market rate, or indeed if capital had to be raised on the market, excessive or frivolous investment would be discouraged.

2. Freedom of entry should be allowed in order to minimize the chance of favorable opportunities being overlooked and to limit the ability of nationalized industries to meet profit targets merely by raising prices in protected markets. Meade notwithstanding, the economies-of-scale argument is intellectually suspect. Abolishing the statutory monopoly enjoyed by the public utilities would allow new entry into profitable lines of business, such as telephone subscriber equipment, intracity postal deliveries, gas and electricity supply. Current restrictions on entry into road and air transport could usefully be relaxed or abolished. Where competition *within* the market is not feasible, competition *for* the market may be possible, for example, by auctioning limited-term franchises for local telephone, gas, and electricity distribution networks, as with local radio and television stations.[82] In many

---

[81] Cf. *The Economist* (London), 24 December 1977, p. 72.
[82] Cf. H. Demsetz, "Why Regulate Utilities?" *Journal of Law and Economics,* April 1968, pp. 55-66.

cases, the mere threat of entry might suffice to promote the competitive process.

3. Instructions to the nationalized industries should be couched in objective rather than subjective terms; that is, they should be operational. Injunctions to set price equal to marginal cost and to appraise investment according to a test discount rate are unenforceable and should therefore be abandoned. In contrast, instructions to break even, or to meet a target rate of net revenue or self-finance, may easily be monitored, as may instructions to provide specified products at specified prices (e.g., a railway service of specified frequency between specified points at a specified maximum rate per mile).

4. It is therefore essential that the government should state explicitly what are the "social obligations" of each nationalized or regulated industry, and how these are to be met, for example, by government subsidy, by cross-subsidy from other consumers, by protection from competition, by cash grants or vouchers to consumers, etc. The government will then be held accountable in Parliament for giving these instructions and ensuring that the industry meets them. Beyond these instructions, the framework within which the industries operate should be designed to make ad hoc government intervention as difficult as possible. Competition has an important role here. Another possibility is to allow industries access to the private capital market. This would provide the necessary funds for those expanding industries, notably telecommunications, which have been severely deprived of capital, while providing some additional pressure to repay on industries like British Steel, which have tended to fall by the wayside.

Political Realities

At this point, one might ask whether any government would be willing to contemplate such a framework for its nationalized industries and, if so, whether there is any point in maintaining their nationalized status. The answer to both questions is probably no. It must be accepted that, in practice, the real purpose and effect of nationalization is not to promote the efficient allocation of resources but precisely the reverse—to prevent it. If this is true, then monopoly is essential and competition is anathema.

This is not by any means to imply that the various motives for nationalization are reprehensible, or that nationalization itself is undesirable—though it may not be the most effective way to achieve the desired ends. Serious conflicts will, however, be generated by failure to acknowledge the *political* considerations and by a framework for control that focuses almost entirely on the issue of efficiency—as indeed events of the past decade have demonstrated.

But even if these political considerations can in some way be resolved, there remain the questions to which the Austrian economists and their followers have addressed themselves, namely, the appropriate role of nationalized industries and the principles upon which they should be operated. Traditional concern about "monopolistic exploitation" in a static framework has diverted attention from the role of competition as a social process of discovering new and better products and techniques. Austrian economists have not been convinced that nationalization is likely to protect consumers from monopoly, much less replace the coordinating process of the competitive market.

New Policy on Nationalized Industries: Austrians Unenthusiastic

A new White Paper, *The Nationalised Industries,*[83] was published after the above section was written. It appears from press accounts (the London *Times,* 6 April 1978) that Ministers are to have powers to issue "specific" directives. This will improve accountability and in that sense is preferable to "arm twisting," but presumably is intended to facilitate detailed government intervention. State industry boards are to be widened to include repre-

[83] *The Nationalised Industries,* Cmnd. 7131 (London: HMSO, March 1978).

sentatives of government and trade unions, management and consumers. This reform recognizes but again increases the power of special interest groups. Financial targets are retained, "tailored to allow for the circumstances of the particular industry," which means they are unlikely to be demanding. The test discount rate is to be replaced by a "required rate of return," but the press account does not succeed in explaining how this differs from the test discount rate and therefore how, if at all, the latter's deficiencies will be avoided. Marginal cost pricing has apparently been allowed to die a quiet death, but "the Government must satisfy itself that the main elements of an industry's pricing structure are sensibly related to costs of supply and market situation." If this is all there is on pricing, it means, in effect, that the government does not know what relationship between price and cost *is* sensible, or is not prepared to say, but nonetheless wishes to preserve the right to intervene. All told, it does not appear to be a document that Austrians will find satisfactory.

VII. Dealing with Externalities

The Prevalence of Externalities

Most decisions concerning location, investment, production, and employment are taken upon agreement of acceptable terms by the parties directly concerned. But economists and the general public have always been aware that one man's action may impose costs and disadvantages on third parties without his having to pay for the damage he does. Such divergences between "private" and "social" consequences are known as "externalities." Increasingly, governments are intervening in an attempt to ensure that these externalities are taken into account.

A glance at a newspaper will suggest the wide range of externalities, leading to situations where government has apparently to resolve a potential dispute.

1. Should a reduction in aircraft noise be secured by improved engine design or by moving airports away from people? —*Times* (London), 17 January 1977.

2. Do the benefits of mining coal in the Vale of Belvoir offset the undesirable effects on the local communities and on the environment? —*Observer* (London), 21 November 1976.

3. Should the site of the Battle of Hastings be sold for property development? —*Times* (London), 12 March 1976.

4. Should an ugly and polluting oil refinery be built at Nigg Point in Scotland where jobs are desired to combat unemployment? —*Times* (London), 3 March 1976.

5. Should betting shops be set up in working-class areas where they are a temptation to the people who live there? —*Wisbech Standard*, 9 January 1976.

57

6. Should farmers be allowed to spray crops by aircraft in view of the danger to beehives and disturbance to householders? —*Times* (London), 5 July 1976.

Alternative Policies

Often no government intervention takes place, either because there is no formal means by which the party disadvantaged may exert influence, or because the effects of some acts are so dispersed or obscure that the detriments are not fully recognized. Where externalities are of lively public concern, a public inquiry may be held, and where they are likely to occur repeatedly, provision for control is often embodied in local or national planning regulations.

Cost-benefit analysis

Economists have developed three main concepts to help in analyzing and treating externalities. The first is social cost-benefit analysis, the aim of which is to identify, evaluate and aggregate the consequences of any action and thereby to choose the solution that maximizes the net benefit to society. To do this, it is necessary to measure the values that people appear to place on commodities such as time, comfort, noise, and pollution, which are seldom traded directly on the market. Notable examples of cost-benefit analysis are the studies of the M-1 motorway, the Victoria underground line, and the Third London Airport.[84]

Externality taxes

A second and somewhat older contribution by economists, dating back to Pigou, is much loved and taught by theorists but so far hardly used in practice. This is the notion of a tax (or subsidy) equal to the divergence between private and social costs or bene-

---

[84] Discussed at greater length in G. H. Peters, *Cost-Benefit Analysis and Public Expenditure,* Institute of Economic Affairs Eaton Paper no. 8, 3rd ed. (London, 1974).

fits. Such a tax imposed on the decision maker would, it is argued, lead him to take the social interest fully into account.

Motorists experience delays in the rush hour, for example, but do not consider the delay they impose upon others by their own contribution to congestion. It is therefore suggested that a rush-hour "congestion tax" be imposed. The Greater London Council is reported to be considering such a tax on large office car parks in Central London, at a rate of, perhaps, £6 per week for each space, in order to reduce peak-period traffic by between 15 and 22 percent.[85] In Singapore, drivers are required to buy special licenses costing about £15 per month in order to drive into the city between 7:30 a.m. and 10:15 a.m. The scheme is said to be an outstanding success with all concerned, since roads in the city center are no longer congested, travel time on buses has been cut by 30 percent, and the government has a steady stream of income.[86]

Economists have also proposed externality taxes on pollution and on noise.[87] Thus, the Civil Aviation Bill currently before Parliament would allow airport authorities to restructure their landing charges so that they discriminate in favor of quieter aircraft.[88] Meade's view, indeed, is that

> the authorities should make a grand tour round the whole economy taxing those activities which are socially costly according to the degree of social costs which they involve.[89]

Property rights

The third main contribution by economists to the debate over externalities is based upon the insight that externalities are intimately related to property rights. Externalities exist because the facilities to make relevant transactions do *not* exist. Developing and enforcing an adequate system of property rights, so that

[85] *Times* (London), 21 February 1976.
[86] World Bank *Report,* May-June 1976, p. 6.
[87] W. Beckerman, *Pricing for Pollution,* Institute of Economic Affairs Hobart Paper no. 66 (London: 1975).
[88] *Times* (London), 16 December 1977.
[89] Meade, *Intelligent Radical's Guide,* p. 113.

people can capture the benefits of "making a market" if it is worth doing so, may obviate the need for frequent and specific government intervention. This approach has been vigorously developed by Coase and Demsetz.[90]

Consider Meade's example of

> the use of nitrates as a fertiliser by farmers, the nitrates finding their way into the neighbourhood's water supply; unless special steps are taken, the farmers will not meet the cost of the damage done to the water supply.[91]

Meade's recommendation is a tax per gallon of pollution or the auction of licenses to pollute up to a given amount per month. But there is a better policy. If the farmers were held legally liable for damages caused by their nitrates, they would have to take these damages into account without any other government intervention.

This solution may be applied to aircraft noise. In Britain, unlike the United States, France, and Germany, citizens no longer have the right to sue for damages.[92] Restoring this right would oblige the airlines and airports authorities to take into account the consequences of aircraft noise when deciding upon airport locations and flight schedules. The convenience of easy airport access in large cities would then have to be offset by the noise inconvenience to a dense population of householders.

The Austrian View

Austrian economists have mostly been preoccupied with economic problems that seemed of more significance than externalities. Nevertheless, one passage by Mises clearly indicates that he anticipated the property rights analysis:

---

[90] R. H. Coase, "The Problem of Social Cost," *Journal of Law and Economics* 3 (1960): 1-44; H. Demsetz, "Toward a Theory of Property Rights," *American Economic Review (Proceedings)*, May 1967, pp. 347-59.

[91] Meade, *Intelligent Radical's Guide*, p. 110.

[92] Letter from Hugh Jenkins, MP, to the *Times* (London), 14 February 1978.

> It is true that where a considerable part of the costs incurred are external costs from the point of view of the acting individuals or firms, the economic calculation established by them is manifestly defective and their results deceptive. But this is not the outcome of alleged deficiencies inherent in the system of private ownership of the means of production. It is on the contrary a consequence of loopholes left in this system. It could be removed by a reform of the laws concerning liability for damages inflicted and by rescinding the institutional barriers preventing the full operation of private ownership.[93]

Why do Austrian ideas suggest the use of property rights rather than the use of cost-benefit analysis or externality taxes? In Austrian thinking, the task is not primarily one of computing the optimal solution to a well-defined "problem," but rather one of discovering the "problem" in the first place (and the possibility of making some improvement), then gathering and utilizing the necessary information, and finally implementing an improved solution.

What kind of institutional framework is most likely to promote the discovery of activities with significant externalities? Will complaints from people affected by aircraft noise be sufficient to alert the appropriate department of national or local government? Or is the prospect of paying and receiving damages more likely to spur the parties to agreement?

How will the information necessary to reach an efficient solution be acquired? In the market, negotiations take place between parties who act in accordance with their own preferences and the opportunities they believe open to them. For an agency carrying out a public inquiry or a cost-benefit analysis, or setting externality taxes, a major difficulty is that these preferences and opportunities must be estimated. If conservationists have to purchase the site of the Battle of Hastings from the property developers, or art lovers a Rembrandt from foreign buyers, these same actions reveal the values placed on these commodities.

Finally, what incentives do the individuals involved in each process have to implement the solution thought to be most efficient? In the market the incentive is private gain; in a bureau-

---

[93] Mises, *Human Action*, pp. 657-8.

cracy other incentives and pressures take precedence. Experience so far suggests that for political reasons it is unlikely that the recommendation of a cost-benefit analysis will be unhesitatingly accepted, or that an externality tax will be imposed at the rate calculated as optimal. The M-1 and Victoria Line studies were completed after the crucial decisions had been made, but the recommendations of studies on the Cambrian Line and the Third London Airport were rejected. Presumably the government attached a *political* significance to the outcomes of the various alternatives which was different from that of the investigating Commission, and probably different again from the view that consumers would have expressed in the market. Specifically, it seems that the government was most concerned to retain popularity with small Welsh coastal towns and potential employers and employees in the neighborhood of Foulness. If this is the fate of the recommendations of a formal public inquiry, it seems unlikely that recommendations about the location of new coal mines and oil refineries, which may be based upon informal analyses by government departments or local authorities, will be any less vulnerable to political pressures. Politicians are in office to respond to public pressures, not to override them.

All this is not to suggest that political pressures are undesirable, or that governments should not respond to them. The argument is, rather, that governments inevitably *will* respond to political pressures. It cannot be assumed that the use of cost-benefit analysis and externality taxes will ensure the remedy of externalities in the manner assumed by many welfare economists. Attempts to improve the framework of property rights within which the market operates may well be more fruitful.

The Creation of Property Rights

Professor Demsetz has suggested that property rights have evolved over time precisely as an efficient social response to the emergence of new externalities.[94] The exact nature of this process

[94]Demsetz, "Toward a Theory of Property Rights."

is not yet well understood. However, this is precisely a topic on which Austrian economics ought to be capable of shedding light, since it is an outstanding example of an "organic" phenomenon.

In Britain, property rights are not usually defined by statute but by a succession of common law judgments on specific cases in the light of legal precedent. Not all decisions are as helpful in defining property rights as one might wish. It was recently held, for example, that the owners of salmon fishing rights in the River Spey do not have the right to prevent public use of the waters for canoeing and sailing.[95] This decision establishes a property right where the situation was not previously well defined, but the resulting property right, being held by "the public," is not transferable. Even if the value of (uninterrupted) salmon fishing were higher than the value of canoeing, it is difficult to see how potential fishermen could buy the right to fish from potential canoeists. Had the legal decision gone the other way, it would have been straightforward for potential canoeists to negotiate with the easily identified owners of the fishing rights. Far from protecting the rights of the public at large, this legal decision may have prevented the use of resources in the way the public would prefer.

The creation of property rights is not a conscious act but rather the unintended consequence of a multitude of actions by people with control over property and by others trying to attain such control. Only gradually over time does the notion of a transferable property right emerge. This insight enables us to appreciate that the apparently chaotic state of affairs in the early days of radio, with transmitting stations in different locations interfering with one another's broadcasts, marked in reality an intermediate stage in the definition of property rights. Those rights, as Coase has argued, were beginning to emerge and would have evolved into an efficient market in radio broadcasting in the United States, had not the government intervened to prevent it.[96]

Similarly, we are seeing today the gradual creation of fishing

[95] House of Lords Law Report, *Times* (London), 3 March 1976.
[96] R. H. Coase, "The Federal Communications Commission," *Journal of Law and Economics,* October 1959, especially pp. 30-31.

rights in the North Sea, in response to conflicts between fishermen of different nations. There has always been an absence of property rights in the sea, as a result of which no one has an incentive to economize stocks of fish through time. Recent developments in fishing technology, such as refrigerated holds, allow longer voyages to more distant waters. The scale of the problem is therefore magnified. What we are now seeing is a vast new enclosure of (private) property in the sea comparable to the enclosure of land in the 18th and 19th centuries.

To establish national fishing quotas in areas nominally open to all European Economic Community nations is one solution that has been advocated. An alternative is to extend the territory of individual countries. "With a 200-mile limit, we could license outsiders to fish in our waters and back this up with a tough fishery protection system," suggested James Johnson, Labour MP for Hull West and chairman of the House of Commons all-party fisheries committee. In other words, if fishing rights can be defined and policed, they can be bought and sold. Such an international market in North Sea fishing rights would provide an incentive to the owners to conserve stocks of fish and at the same time allow the fishing to be undertaken by those with the lowest costs.

VIII. National Economic Planning in Britain

Britain's Industrial Strategy

"The task we face," wrote Denis Healey, the British Chancellor of the Exchequer, and Eric Varley, the Secretary of State for Industry, "is nothing less than to reverse the relative decline of British industry which has been continuous for many years."[97]

To achieve this task, the 1975 Industry Act introduced two "powerful new instruments": planning agreements with major firms in key sectors of industry, and the National Enterprise Board (NEB) to provide the means for "direct public initiatives" (e.g., making investments or buying shareholdings) in key sectors.

Planning Agreements

Advocates of the mixed economy frequently argue that the market price mechanism is inefficient because it lacks a complete system of contingent forward markets. Meade has asked:

> In the absence of a futures market, how can the total plans of all the steel producers to supply steel in the future be coordinated with the total plans of all the steel users to use steel in the future?[98]

The National Economic Development Council was created in 1961 to bring together various people in a "process of consultation and forecasting with a view to better coordination of ideas

[97] *An Approach to Industrial Strategy,* Cmnd. 6315 (London: HMSO, November 1975), p. 3 (Foreword); *The Regeneration of British Industry,* Cmnd. 5710 (London: HMSO, August 1974).

[98] Meade, *Intelligent Radical's Guide,* p. 104.

and plans." The idea was to develop some form of "indicative planning," in "an attempt to promote more stable, rapid and efficient growth via the exchange of forecasts, leading to a generally held set of consistent expectations."[99] A process of repeated consultation, it was argued, would remove uncertainties associated with the actions of other market participants. Firms can produce more efficiently knowing that their supplies and markets are secure, bottlenecks and other obstacles to growth can be identified and remedied, and all market participants may be induced to revise upwards their expectations and plans for economic growth.

Failure of Planning in the 1960s

The attempts to put indicative planning into practice in the 1960s did not meet these expectations and were abandoned within the decade.[100] What went wrong? Was the attempt doomed to failure? *"Mainstream" economic theory can shed little light on the problem.* A framework of general equilibrium which assumes perfect knowledge cannot hope to explain a situation whose very essence is *lack* of knowledge. In contrast, this is precisely the framework of uncertainty within which Austrian economics has developed. From this vantage point, two potential difficulties with indicative planning immediately appear.

First, it is assumed that each firm will "play the game" by stating truthfully its own plans. A firm's incentive to comply with the Plan is that it incorporates the firm's own stated plans. But if the method of competition is to take competitors by surprise, any one firm has an incentive to mislead others and to *conceal* its true plans. Since there is a cost to participating in the national planning process, a firm might wonder how much time and expense it is really worthwhile to invest in such an artificial exercise.

---

[99] J. Black, "Theory of Indicative Planning," *Oxford Economic Papers,* November 1968.

[100] An incisive critique of Britain's first national plan may be found in J. Brunner, *The National Plan,* Institute of Economic Affairs Eaton Paper no. 4, 3rd ed. (London, 1969).

Second, firms cannot hope to commit themselves to plans for five years ahead. Even if the plans of suppliers and competitors are known, the uncertainties associated with external events cannot be removed. New technological developments will inevitably occur, and there is no convenient way of introducing the views of final consumers, even if they could be supposed to make consumption plans for five years ahead. Even the best-laid plans eventually have to be revised.

In proposing flexible planning agreements, the British government now appears to have recognized the necessity to cope with change.

> The likelihood is that any plan which erected a single complete and mutually consistent set of industrial forecasts would rapidly be falsified by events and have to be discarded.[101]

Planning agreements are to be concluded individually between the government and major firms in key industrial sectors. They will be drawn up for three years ahead, reviewed, and rolled forward annually. It is envisaged that firms will supply past data, forecasts, long-term plans, and changes in plans on investment, prices, productivity, employment, exports and import saving, "interests of consumers and the community," etc. Since the government does not wish to restrict firms' freedom to respond to market changes, the agreements will not be enforceable at law.

But how useful is a *flexible* plan? The advantage of a coordinated plan is precisely to *commit* each party to a specific line of action. If flexibility is introduced, this advantage will no longer hold: Each party will have to make its own estimates of how external events will turn out and how other parties will respond. What, then, do firms or the government gain from planning agreements? In a world of uncertainty, national plans and planning agreements can achieve coordination only at the expense of freedom to initiate and respond to change. *Far from supplementing the market process, national planning precludes it.*

Lest there be any confusion here, it should be emphasized that the above argument is not directed against "planning" per se. It is

---

[101] *An Approach to Industrial Strategy*, p. 7.

clearly necessary that private firms, nationalized industries, and government departments all make "plans," and flexible ones at that, *within their appropriate spheres.* "National planning" is a horse of a different color altogether. The real question is not whether planning should take place, but who is to do the planning.[102]

The National Enterprise Board

The NEB was set up with an initial capital of £500 million (subsequently doubled) to provide investment capital, promote reorganization of industries by taking shareholdings, manage existing government shareholdings, assist ailing companies, create employment, and provide a source of financial and managerial advice. Like its predecessor, the Industrial Reorganization Corporation (IRC), the NEB was established in the belief that mergers needed to be arranged between many firms or factories too small to reap the benefits of economies of scale and that new investments needed to be made in many firms using outdated techniques or equipment. "There is no evidence," said the White Paper on the IRC in 1966,[103] "that we can rely on market forces alone to provide the necessary structural changes at the pace required." There were many financial institutions "but there is no organisation whose special function is to search for opportunities to promote rationalisation schemes which could yield benefits to the whole economy."

This assertion betrayed a naive misunderstanding of the market mechanism. Every shareholder, every entrepreneur, every manager has direct financial incentive to identify activities where improvements might be made. If a bottleneck is not identified until too late, a firm loses money; by the same token, profits could have been made by anticipating the bottleneck. Firms go to whatever lengths they deem appropriate to secure their supplies:

---

[102]Cf. Hayek, "The New Confusion about 'Planning,'" *Morgan Guarantee Survey,* January 1976 (reprinted in his *New Studies*).
[103]*Industrial Reorganization Corporation,* Cmnd. 2889 (London: HMSO, January 1966).

Sometimes they buy ahead, sometimes they integrate back into the supply industry, at yet other times they find it more profitable to take a risk and modify their plans as the situation develops.

If the future were known, there would be little difficulty in identifying the optimal structure of each industry and the optimal set of techniques. But in that event, the problems would not arise in the first place. The question to be posed is whether the NEB can expect to make *better* predictions and decisions than the thousands of individuals in the market. It seems unlikely. Participants in the market have collectively not only more experience and knowledge but also the personal financial incentive to seek out relevant information and to make correct decisions. Over time the market encourages people who are successful and weeds out those who are not. By contrast, members of the NEB are not risking their own money and are under pressure to return an overall performance which is satisfactory to the government. And for the government, profit derived from efficiency and alertness is only one of many considerations—political considerations may count for more. Thus, it has been explicitly stated that the purpose of the NEB is "to secure where necessary large-scale sustained investment to offset the effects of the short-term pull of market forces.[104] This presumably means that the NEB should act to promote employment or prevent unemployment, to increase exports or replace imports, to build up a large domestic concern, or to prevent foreign control.

"Burning the Furniture to Heat the Stove": The British Approach?

The owners and employees of a firm that receives financial assistance or preferential treatment will usually benefit from it. But such actions have a cost in opportunities foregone: Funds have to be withdrawn from some other use, or prices are maintained at a higher level than they otherwise would be. Now the economist qua economist cannot object to the redistribution of income from tax-

---

[104] *The Regeneration of British Industry.*

payers and consumers to owners and employees of firms in actual or potential financial difficulties. For humanitarian reasons, he may support a program designed to cushion the effects of change. He must object, however, to the *pretense* that this will reverse the decline in British industry, and he may even question whether those whom such a policy is intended to benefit will, in the long run, be better off. Here again the Austrian view, put by Mises, is relevant to our present day:

> There are certainly, both in the actions of individuals and in the conduct of public affairs, situations in which the actors may have good reasons to put up even with very undesirable long-run effects in order to avoid what they consider still more undesirable short-run conditions. It may sometimes be expedient for a man to heat the stove with his furniture. But if he does, he should know what the remoter effects will be. He should not delude himself by believing that he has discovered a wonderful new method of heating his premises.[105]

The debate about national planning reveals in particularly stark form the fallacies that the Austrians have been most concerned to expose. The prime defense of national planning has not been the desirability of protecting any particular social group or promoting the consumption of any particular product, nor has it been the need to curb the activities of powerful firms or unions. The claim has been, instead, that national planning, in one or more of its variants, can "reverse the decline of British industry" by increasing the efficiency with which the economy operates. Ultimately, the basis for this claim is that government, or one of its agencies, has a better knowledge of what needs to be done, at least in general terms if not in detail, than do the many thousands of individual firms in the economy.

Now it is clear that firms in the market are continually making errors of omission and commission, which they could avoid if they had better knowledge, which would lead in turn to a much faster growth rate in the economy. What is not explained is how the government has or is able to acquire the superior knowledge that will make this possible. Does the government have a different source of knowledge from that of the firms? If so, what is it? Or is

[105]Mises, *Human Action*, p. 654.

its knowledge merely a synthesis of what it learns from firms? If so, how does it reduce the total quantity of information to a manageable level, sort out the wheat from the chaff, and resolve the inevitable ambiguities and conflicts in the information received? No settled answers to these questions are forthcoming.

Austrians have long been clear about the issues involved. The practical impossibility of efficient central planning has been frequently dissected by Hayek, most recently in 1976:

> . . . the economic order of any large society rests on a utilisation of the knowledge of particular circumstances widely dispersed among thousands or millions of individuals.
>
> . . . the market and the competitive determination of prices have provided a procedure by which it is possible to convey to the individual managers of productive units as much information in condensed form as they need in order to fit their plans into the order of the rest of the system.
>
> The alternative of having all the individual managers of businesses convey to a central planning authority the knowledge of particular facts which they possess is clearly impossible—simply because they never can know beforehand which of the many concrete circumstances about which they have knowledge or could find out might be of importance to the central planning authority.[106]

For similar reasons, the planning agreements and the NEB cannot hope to improve upon the efficiency in the use of resources which the market makes possible.

[106]Hayek, "The New Confusion about 'Planning.' "

IX. Summing Up

The Distinctive Austrian Approach

Mises believed that the ideas of the original Austrian school founded by Carl Menger in 1870 were substantially incorporated into "mainstream" economic theory by 1920. The work of the second and third generation Austrians, notably Mises himself and Hayek, has not been so incorporated. Their ideas have been subsequently developed by Kirzner, Lachmann, Rothbard, and others who, although not Austrian by birth, may be considered members of the Austrian School. In addition, I have argued that about a dozen other noted scholars, working independently, have been directly or indirectly influenced by Mises or Hayek and that their work is substantially in sympathy with that of the Austrian School.

Austrian economic theory is based upon the twin principles of methodological individualism and subjectivism. Economic phenomena must be related to the actions of the *individuals* involved, which in turn must be interpreted in terms of their purposes and perceived opportunities. These two principles both describe what Austrian economists do and define what Austrians believe good economics to be. These principles also provide a kind of guideline by which to evaluate a situation or theory.

Neoclassical "mainstream" economics pays lip service to these principles. The working of the competitive economy is supposedly "explained" in terms of the choices of individual firms and consumers, determined by their preferences and resources. But these choices are made in the light of *perfect information;* there is no explanation of *how* all prices come to be known and consequently *how* a competitive equilibrium comes about.

73

Austrian economics takes as its starting point the behavior of people with incomplete knowledge, who have not only to "economize" in the situations in which they find themselves, but also to be on the alert for better opportunities "just around the corner." This alertness, missing from "mainstream" economics, is called entrepreneurship. It leads to the revision of plans and forms the basis of the competitive process, which in many ways epitomizes the Austrian approach. For Austrians, the *changes* over time in prices, production, plans, knowledge, and expectations are more important than prices and output at any one time. Similarly, from a "normative" point of view (of what policy should be), the adequacy of an economic system is judged not by the efficiency with which it allocates given resources at a point in time, but by the speed with which it discovers and responds to new opportunities over time.

"Mainstream" economics has approached the role of government by identifying as "market failures" situations in which "perfect competition" is not possible. But very often the alleged failure is due to a *lack of information*, in which case government intervention cannot hope to perform any better. Moreover, the incentives for the members of government organizations are different from those of private organizations, in a way which is not likely to improve the former's performance.

The Implications for Government Policy

These ideas have been illustrated in this discussion by examination of British government policies on competition, nationalized industries, externalities, and national planning. The conclusions have been broadly that, in all these contexts, the present extent of government intervention cannot be justified if the aim is to encourage an efficient, responsive, and increasingly wealthy economy. Even the "intelligent radical" who places a high value on liberty and equality would not, we have argued, favor the "mixed economy" advocated on his behalf by Meade. We have found that the free-market economy is surprisingly resilient, that it has strengths in an environment of uncertainty and change which are not appreciated if perfect knowledge is assumed, and that government intervention has corresponding weaknesses. A more effective way of achieving the desired ends would be to promote the competitive process by removing government-imposed barriers to new entry and by strengthening the system of private property rights.

In more detail the implications of these policy changes are mainly four:

1. It was suggested that the Monopolies and Mergers Commission should no longer be responsible for mergers. This would make it easier for efficient large firms to expand and would withdraw protection from firms whose assets are not being used as efficiently as they might be. Patent monopolies should be abolished. This would expose the established companies in industries such as, notably, pharmaceuticals and computers to active competition from new and smaller firms able to produce more efficiently or to make minor improvements on established products. Consumers would benefit from cheaper products, although more fundamental discoveries, at least in those industries, might possibly be introduced more slowly. Finally, relaxing the laws against restrictive practices might allow the continuation of collusions to raise prices by electrical and construction firms. On the other hand, removing the statutory monopoly power of the professions would put an end to the present scandal of conveyancing charges.

2. Allowing competition against the nationalized industries and enforcing financial discipline there would no doubt lead to more rapid closures of inefficient steelworks and pits by British Steel and the National Coal Board. It is possible, however, that some of this labor would be taken on by expanding private firms in those sectors. The postal side of the Post Office would certainly contract but the telecommunications side would expand. Consumers would benefit from lower prices for telephone calls and from competition to provide more attractive and efficient telephone sets. British Rail and the aircraft and shipbuilding industries would contract more rapidly. Indeed, the size of the public sector generally would be reduced, but the shift in demand and

resources to the private sector would lead to expansion there more or less across the board.

3. Abandoning government inquiries into controversies about planning permission does not necessarily mean that externalities would be ignored, leading to increased pollution, noise, and scenic devastation. It was recommended that private property rights be better defined and enforced, so that these less tangible goods can be transacted in the market. If airlines have to compensate residents in the neighborhood of airports for excessive noise levels, it is much more likely than now that the airlines will take notice. The same is true of water and air pollution. It does of course raise the question whether conservationists will be able to raise sufficient funds to protect the scenery, or persuade taxpayers to do so. If not, this would indicate that scenic delights are a minority interest. That the National Trust has been able steadily to increase its purchase of Britain's coastline suggests that all is by no means lost for conservationists and nature lovers.

4. Finally, to abandon the attempt to sign planning agreements would remove a potential hindrance from the larger firms, and to sell back the assets of the NEB to private industry would mean less help was available for firms in distress. Employees and shareholders in such industries would suffer, at least initially, but consumers and taxpayers would benefit.

The general effect of adopting these Austrian proposals is that resources would tend to be used as consumers, given their incomes, wished. The result would not necessarily be compatible with any particular person's idea of "social justice," but a responsive and growing economy provides the best likelihood of satisfying the wishes of people in general.

The Limitations of Government

Adopting the recommendations of Austrian economists would not immediately solve Britain's economic problems. Though many people would benefit, others would initially experience serious and unpleasant changes in their lives. But this fate, of course, is precisely what successive governments of both political complexions have been predicting over the past decade. Without exception they have seen our salvation in a larger role for government. And without exception it has failed.

Why then do we still persevere with a mixed economy? There are basically two reasons. The first is intellectual: Most people in politics and academia and the general public have been genuinely persuaded that a mixed economy is necessary and inevitable. Indeed, as the modern economy grows more complex, it is thought necessary to extend the role of government. One of the purposes of this discussion has been to show how Austrian ideas explode this myth. In Hayek's words:

> . . . the complexity of the structure required to produce the real income we are now able to provide for the masses of the Western world—which exceeds anything we can survey or picture in detail—could develop *only* because we did *not* attempt to plan it or subject it to any central direction, but left it to be guided by a spontaneous ordering mechanism, or a self-generating order, as modern cybernetics calls it.[107]

This understanding of the vital role of organic, as opposed to pragmatic, institutions is characteristic of Austrians. Hayek expresses the theme in more general terms:

> We flatter ourselves undeservedly if we represent human civilization as entirely the product of conscious reason or as the product of human design, or when we assume that it is necessarily in our power deliberately to re-create or to maintain what we have built without knowing what we were doing.
>
> Though our civilization is the result of a cumulation of individual knowledge, it is not by the explicit or conscious combination of all this knowledge in any individual brain, but by its embodiment in symbols which we use without understanding them, in habits and institutions, tools and concepts, that man in society is constantly able to profit from a body of knowledge neither he nor any other man completely possesses.
>
> Many of the greatest things man has achieved are not the result of consciously directed thought, and still less the product of a deliberately coordinated effort of many individuals, but of a process in which the individual plays a part which he can never fully understand. They are greater than any individual precisely because they result from the combination of knowledge more extensive than a single mind can master.[108]

---

[107] Hayek, "The New Confusion about 'Planning.'"
[108] Hayek, *Counter-Revolution of Science,* p. 84.

This appraisal leads to an appreciation of the necessarily modest role of government.

> If man is not to do more harm than good in his efforts to improve the social order, he will have to learn that . . . where essential complexity of an organized kind prevails, *he cannot acquire the full knowledge which would make mastery of the events possible.* He will therefore have to use what knowledge he can achieve, not to shape the results as the craftsman shapes his handiwork, but rather to cultivate a growth by providing the appropriate environment, as the gardener does for his plants.[109] (My italics.)

The Political Problem of Democracy

The second reason advanced for the continuation and extension of the mixed economy is political. As any politician will confirm, it would be political suicide to resist it. The explanation is not difficult to find. Although the various aspects of direct government intervention discussed above cannot be justified as in the interests of people as a whole, it is undoubtedly true that each measure, taken separately, benefits at least one group of people. Prohibitions on mergers protect competitors and employees likely to be made redundant as capacity is rationalized. Nationalization slows down the rate at which resources are transferred out of declining industries, thereby benefiting their employees and sometimes their consumers. If the NEB invests in a firm when others are unwilling to do so, the benefits to its shareholders and employees are obvious. It may, indeed, be argued that the various devices of government involvement in industry are deliberately intended to serve the interests of powerful political groups. It is political pressures that provide the initial impetus for such measures and the support to carry them through.

By no means as obvious are the disadvantages imposed on others. If consumers of one product or employees in one industry are favored, it is necessarily at the expense of consumers of other products, of employees in other industries, or of taxpayers generally. Support and protection for one industry can be given only

[109] Hayek, "The Pretense of Knowledge."

by reducing support for another, in effect diverting resources away from uses to which consumers would have preferred to direct them.

This diagnosis of the nature of knowledge poses ultimately the political problem of democracy. Even if all citizens as consumers stand to gain from a general policy of nonintervention, each citizen as employee or investor stands to gain from *particular* interventions. The dilemma has been examined by Hayek, Rothbard, and others, who have shown how this and other problems of democracy are inherent in a system that must respond to the shifting dictates of pressure-group politics.[110]

The development of Austrian thought on the borders of economics and political science forms an appropriate conclusion to this discussion. The gradual and insidious encroachment of the mixed economy is a direct but unintended consequence of our political system. The quite different government policy which the "intelligent radical" would derive from an application of Austrian economics may seem unlikely to be widely acceptable today. But the Austrian contribution depends squarely upon the phenomenon of learning from experience. The Austrian must be confident that even ideas at present unthinkable will eventually be accepted, and sooner rather than later.

Having revealed the theoretical flaw and thus the root fallacy of the mixed economy, Austrian economics offers the prospect of government policy that would much more certainly achieve the aspirations of the "intelligent radical."

[110]F. A. Hayek, *Law, Legislation and Liberty: The Mirage of Social Justice* (Chicago: University of Chicago Press, 1977) and his *Economic Freedom and Representative Government;* M. N. Rothbard, *Power and Market: Government and the Economy* , 2nd ed. (Kansas City: Sheed Andrews and McMeel, 1977), pp. 189-99; J. M. Buchanan, *The Limits of Liberty: Between Anarchy and Leviathan* (Chicago: University of Chicago Press, 1975); Lord Hailsham, *The Dilemma of Democracy: Diagnosis and Prescription* (London: Collins, 1978).

RECOMMENDED READING

A good introduction to modern Austrian economics is a set of lectures given by Kirzner, Lachmann, and Rothbard at a conference in South Royalton, Vermont, in 1974:

Dolan, E. G., ed. *The Foundations of Modern Austrian Economics.* Kansas City: Sheed & Ward, 1976.

Hayek's recent lectures constitute an elegant and hard-hitting statement of Austrian views on current government policy toward inflation:

Hayek, F. A. *Unemployment and Monetary Policy: Government as Generator of the "Business Cycle."* Cato Paper no. 3. San Francisco: Cato Institute, 1979.

The "classics" of Austrian economics most pertinent to the topic of this *Cato Paper* are as follows:

Menger, C. *Principles of Economics* (1871). Translated by J. Dingwall and B. Hoselitz. Glencoe, Ill.: Free Press, 1950.

———. *Problems of Economics and Sociology* (1883). Translated by F. J. Nock. Edited by L. Schneider. Urbana: University of Illinois Press, 1960.

Mises, L. von. *Human Action: A Treatise on Economics.* 3rd rev. ed. Chicago: Regnery, 1963.

Hayek, F. A. *The Counter-Revolution of Science: Studies on the Abuse of Reason.* New York: Free Press, 1952.

———. *Individualism and Economic Order.* Chicago: University of Chicago Press, 1948. Two of the most important articles reprinted in this volume are "Economics and Knowledge," *Economica* 4 (1937):33-54; and "The Use of Knowledge in Society," *American Economic Review* 35 (1945):519-30. Their full significance for economic theory and policy, respectively, has not yet been widely appreciated.

A minor Austrian classic is a short paper which argues that the market will prevail over the state:

Böhm-Bawerk, E. von. "Control or Economic Law?" In *Shorter Classics of Eugen von Böhm-Bawerk.* South Holland, Ill.: Libertarian Press, 1962.

Many of Lachmann's perceptive and very readable contributions are unfortunately widely scattered but have recently been collected into one volume:

Lachmann, L. M. *Capital, Expectations, and the Market Process: Essays on the Theory of the Market Economy.* Kansas City: Sheed Andrews & McMeel, 1977.

A comprehensive treatise on economic principles, heavily influenced by Mises's *Human Action* and aimed at the beginner, is:

Rothbard, M. N. *Man, Economy, and State: A Treatise on Economic Principles.* New York: Van Nostrand, 1962.

An excellent (but out-of-print) intermediate textbook that integrates the Austrian theory of market process with the neoclassical "mainstream" approach is:

Kirzner, I. M. *Market Theory and the Price System.* New York: Van Nostrand, 1963.

In my opinion one of the most important contributions to microeconomics of the last quarter-century is:

Kirzner, I. M. *Competition and Entrepreneurship.* Chicago: University of Chicago Press, 1973.

Other Highly Recommended Works

Alchian, A. *Economic Forces at Work,* pp. 273-334. Indianapolis. Liberty Press, 1977.

Buchanan, J. M. *Cost and Choice.* Chicago: Markham, 1969.

Buchanan, J. M., and Thirlby, G. F. *L.S.E. Essays on Cost.* London: Weidenfeld and Nicolson, 1973.

Fetter, F.A. *Capital, Interest, and Rent: Essays in the Theory of Distribution.* Kansas City: Sheed Andrews & McMeel, 1977.

Hayek, F. A. *Monetary Theory and the Trade Cycle.* Clifton, N.J.: Kelley, 1975.

————. *New Studies in Philosophy, Politics, Economics, and the History of Ideas.* Chicago: University of Chicago Press, 1978.

————. *Prices and Production.* Clifton, N.J.: Kelley, 1967.

————. *Profits, Interest and Investment, and Other Essays on the Theory of Industrial Fluctuations.* Clifton, N.J.: Kelley, 1975.

————. *A Tiger by the Tail: The Keynesian Legacy of Inflation.* Cato Paper no. 7. San Francisco: Cato Institute, 1979.

Hayek, F. A., ed. *Collectivist Economic Planning*. Clifton, N.J.: Kelley, 1975.

Kirzner, I. M. *An Essay on Capital*. New York: Kelley, 1966.

Lachmann, L. M. *Capital and Its Structure*. Kansas City: Sheed Andrews & McMeel, 1978.

O'Driscoll, G. P., Jr. *Economics as a Coordination Problem: The Contributions of Friedrich A. Hayek*. Kansas City: Sheed Andrews & McMeel, 1977.

Rizzo, M. J., ed. *Time, Uncertainty, and Disequilibrium: Exploration on Austrian Themes*. Lexington, Mass.: Heath, 1979.

Rothbard, M. N. *Power and Market: Government and the Economy*. Kansas City: Sheed Andrews & McMeel, 1978.

——. *Toward a Reconstruction of Utility and Welfare Economics*. New York: Center for Libertarian Studies, 1977.

Spadaro, L. M., ed. *New Directions in Austrian Economics*. Kansas City: Sheed Andrews & McMeel, 1978.

Wicksteed, P. H. *The Common Sense of Political Economy*. London: Macmillan, 1910.

Wieser, F. von. "The Theory of Value." *Annals of the American Academy of Political and Social Science* 2 (March 1892).

ABOUT THE AUTHOR

Stephen Littlechild received a Bachelor of Commerce degree from the University of Birmingham in 1964 and his Ph.D. from the University of Texas at Austin in 1969. His postgraduate and post-doctoral studies included operations research and economics at Stanford and Northwestern universities, and at the University of California, Los Angeles.

Littlechild was formerly Assistant Lecturer in Industrial Economics at the University of Birmingham (1964-65), Senior Research Lecturer in Economics at the Graduate Centre for Management Studies (1970-73), and Professor of Applied Economics at the University of Aston (1973-75). Since 1975 he has been Professor of Commerce at the University of Birmingham. He has been a consultant to the British Ministry of Transport, the British Treasury, the World Bank, General Motors, and American Telephone and Telegraph Co.

Littlechild is the editor and coauthor of *Operational Research for Managers.* He is a contributor to *New Directions in Austrian Economics* (ed. L. M. Spadaro) and *Pricing in Regulated Industries: Theory and Application* (ed. J. Wenders). His articles and reviews have appeared in *Bell Journal of Economics; Economic Journal; Journal of Economic Theory; Journal of Public Economics; Metroeconomica; Review of Economic Studies,* and elsewhere.